OFFICIAL SQA PAST PAPERS WITH ANSWERS

STANDARD GRADE | GENERAL

PHYSICS
2008-2012

 SQA

 BrightRED PUBLISHING

© Scottish Qualifications Authority
All rights reserved. Copying prohibited. No part of this publication may be reproduced, stored in a retrieval system, or transmitted in any form or by any means, electronic, mechanical, photocopying, recording or otherwise.

First exam published in 2008.
Published by Bright Red Publishing Ltd, 6 Stafford Street, Edinburgh EH3 7AU
tel: 0131 220 5804 fax: 0131 220 6710 info@brightredpublishing.co.uk www.brightredpublishing.co.uk

ISBN 978-1-84948-256-1

A CIP Catalogue record for this book is available from the British Library.

Bright Red Publishing is grateful to the copyright holders, as credited on the final page of the Question Section, for permission to use their material. Every effort has been made to trace the copyright holders and to obtain their permission for the use of copyright material. Bright Red Publishing will be happy to receive information allowing us to rectify any error or omission in future editions.

STANDARD GRADE | GENERAL

2008

[BLANK PAGE]

FOR OFFICIAL USE

K & U   PS

Total Marks

3220/401

NATIONAL
QUALIFICATIONS
2008

FRIDAY, 23 MAY
9.00 AM – 10.30 AM

PHYSICS
STANDARD GRADE
General Level

G

Fill in these boxes and read what is printed below.

Full name of centre

Town

Forename(s)

Surname

Date of birth
Day Month Year

Scottish candidate number

Number of seat

Reference may be made to the Physics Data Booklet.

1 All questions should be answered.

2 The questions may be answered in any order but all answers must be written clearly and legibly in this book.

3 For questions 1–5, write down, in the space provided, the letter corresponding to the answer you think is correct. There is only **one** correct answer.

4 For questions 6–20, write your answer where indicated by the question or in the space provided after the question.

5 If you change your mind about your answer you may score it out and replace it in the space provided at the end of the answer book.

6 Before leaving the examination room you must give this book to the invigilator. If you do not, you may lose all the marks for this paper.

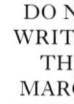

Marks

1. When a student whistles a note into a microphone connected to an oscilloscope, the following pattern is displayed.

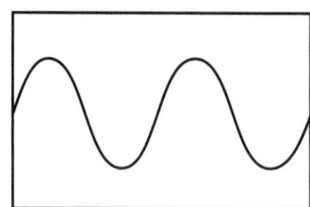

Without changing the oscilloscope controls, another student whistles a quieter note of higher frequency into the microphone. Which of the following shows the pattern which would be displayed on the screen?

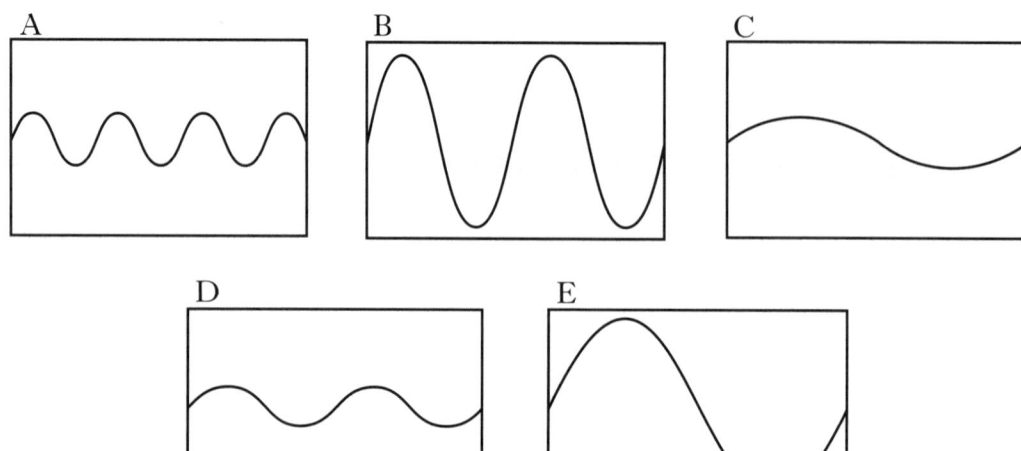

Answer ☐   1

2. The weather information satellite NOAA-15 has a period of 99 minutes and an orbital height of 833 kilometres.

The geostationary weather information satellite Meteosat has a period of 1440 minutes and an orbital height of 35 900 kilometres.

Which of the following gives the period of a satellite that has an orbital height of 20 000 kilometres?

A   83 minutes

B   99 minutes

C   720 minutes

D 1440 minutes

E 1750 minutes

Answer ☐   1

3. Which row in the table describes the correct configuration for an atom?

	orbiting the nucleus	inside the nucleus
A	protons only	electrons and neutrons
B	electrons and protons	neutrons only
C	neutrons and protons	electrons only
D	electrons only	neutrons and protons
E	neutrons only	electrons and protons

Answer ☐   1

4. The time taken for light to reach us from the Sun is approximately

   A   1 second

   B   8 seconds

   C   1 minute

   D   8 minutes

   E   1 hour.

Answer ☐   1

5. Two objects are dropped from the same height. Both objects fall freely.

Object X has a mass of 10 kilograms.

Object Y has a mass of 1 kilogram.

Object X accelerates at 10 metres per second per second.

The acceleration of object Y, in metres per second per second, is

   A   0·1

   B   1·0

   C   10

   D   100

   E   1000.   Answer ☐   1

[Turn over

DO N
WRITI
THI
MAR(

K&U

Marks

6. A student is listening to a radio.

(*a*) Complete the passage below using words from the following list.

sound	**amplifier**	**light**	**microphone**	
aerial	**battery**	**tuner**	**decoder**	**electrical**

The .... of a radio receiver detects signals from many different stations and converts them into electrical signals.

The .... selects one particular station from many.

The .... increases the amplitude of these electrical signals.

The energy required to do this is supplied by the ....

The loudspeaker in a radio receiver converts .... energy into

.... energy.

3

Marks

6. (continued)

(*b*) Electrical signals are displayed as waves on an oscilloscope.

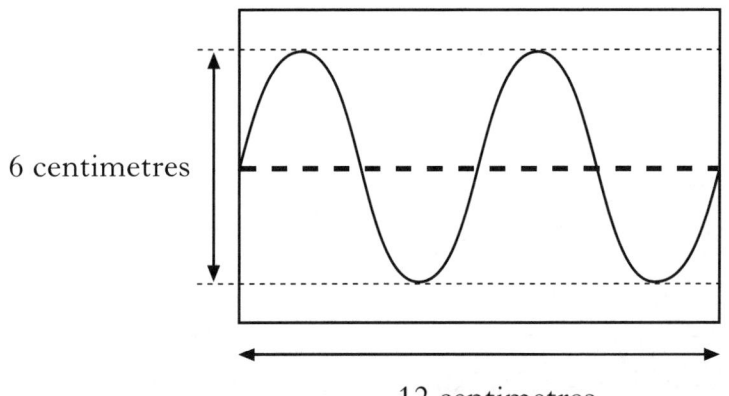

6 centimetres

12 centimetres

(i) Calculate the wavelength of the waves.

> *Space for working and answer*

1

(ii) Calculate the amplitude of the waves.

> *Space for working and answer*

1

[Turn over

DO N
WRIT
TH
MAR

K&U

Marks

7. A football match is being broadcast live from Dundee. Signals from the football stadium are transmitted to a television studio in Glasgow via a relay station on top of a nearby hill.

At the relay station, a curved reflector is placed behind a detector of the television signals.

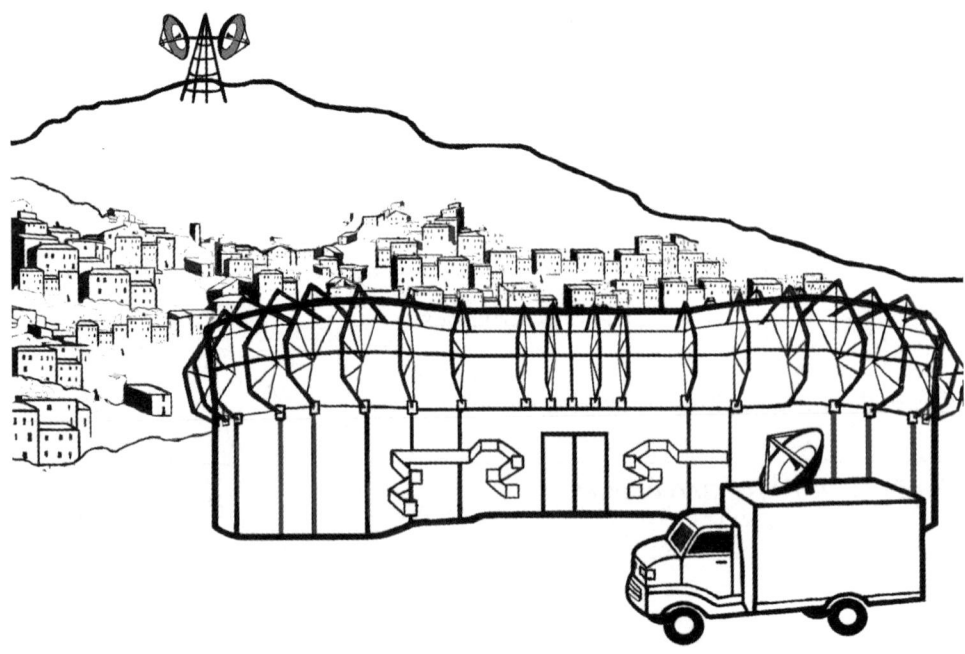

(a) (i) State the purpose of the curved reflector.

.... 1

(ii) Complete the diagram below to show the effect of the curved reflector on the signal at the relay station.

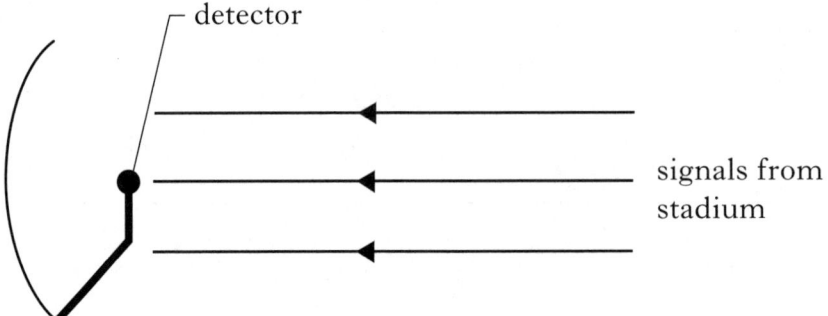

2

Marks

7. (continued)

(*b*) During the match, strong winds cause the reflector to move to a new position as shown.

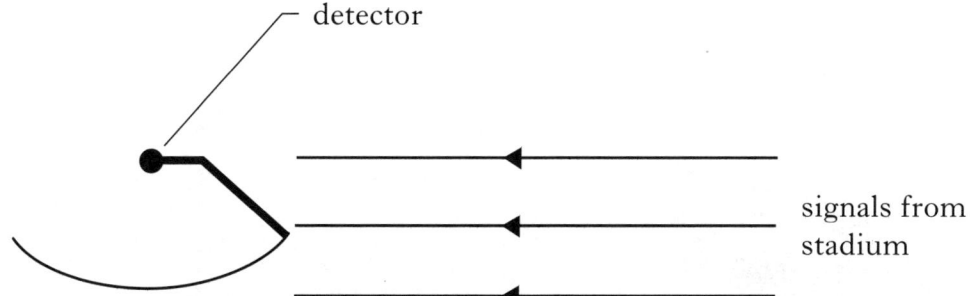

State the effect this has on the signal received at the detector.

.... **1**

[Turn over

Marks

8. Two household electrical appliances, a 1500 watt electric iron and a 300 watt uplighter lamp, are shown below.

electric iron   **uplighter lamp**

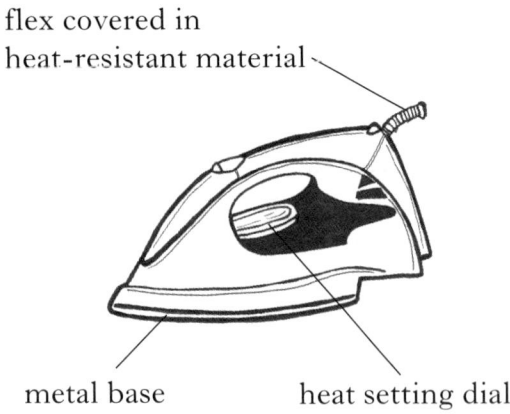

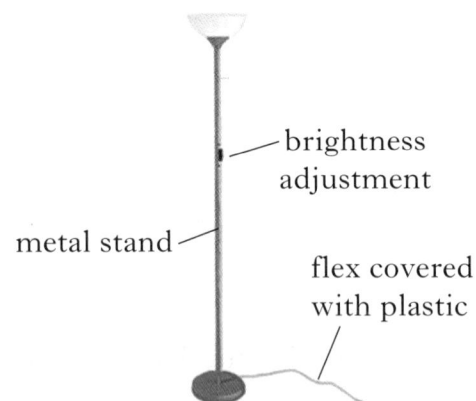

(a) The brightness of the uplighter lamp can be changed.

State an electrical component that could be used to change the brightness of the uplighter lamp.

.... 1

(b) Explain why the flex for the iron is covered with a heat-resistant material.

.... 1

K&U   PS

Marks

8.   (continued)

(*c*)   A cross-section of the flex for each appliance is shown.

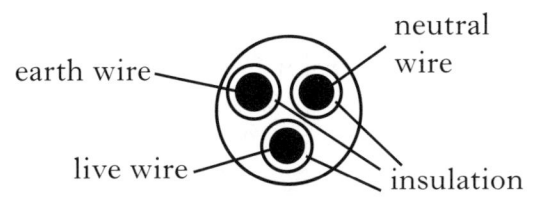

electric iron

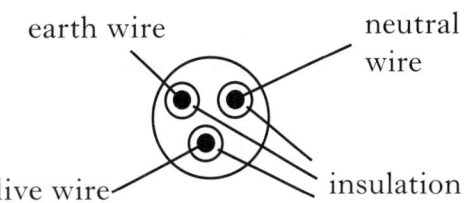

uplighter lamp

(i)   State the colour of the insulation on the live wire.

....   1

(ii)   State the purpose of the earth wire.

....   1

(iii)   Explain why the wires in the flex for the electric iron are thicker than those for the uplighter lamp.

....   1

[Turn over

Marks

9. Two identical lamps are connected to a 6·0 volt battery as shown in circuit 1.

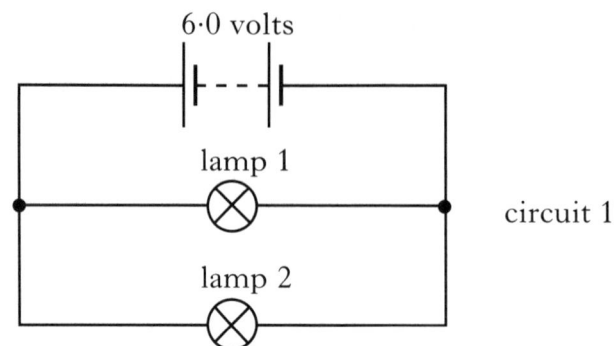

(a) The battery supplies a current of 0·40 ampere to the circuit.

Complete the following table to show the current in each lamp and the voltage across each lamp.

	Lamp 1	Lamp 2
Current (amperes)		
Voltage (volts)		

2

(b) The two lamps are now connected as shown in circuit 2.

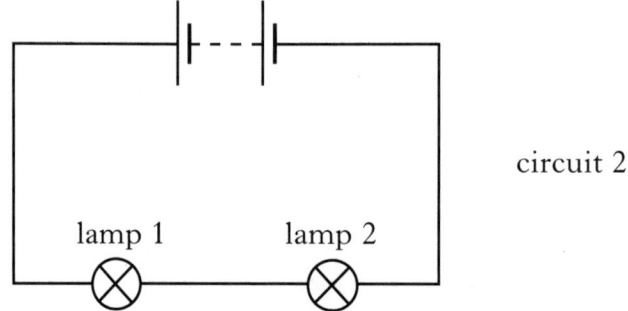

State the voltage of the battery required to light the lamps with the same brightness as in circuit 1.

....   1

(c) In which of the two circuits, circuit 1 or circuit 2, would lamp 2 still be on when lamp 1 is removed?

....   1

DO NOT WRITE IN THIS MARGIN

K&U PS

Marks

10. (*a*) A drummer in a rock band is exposed to sound levels of up to 110 decibels.

Explain why ear protectors are used to reduce the sound level experienced by the drummer.

.... **1**

(*b*) A medical researcher is measuring the upper range of hearing of people in different age groups.

The bar graph shows the frequencies of sound detected by these people.

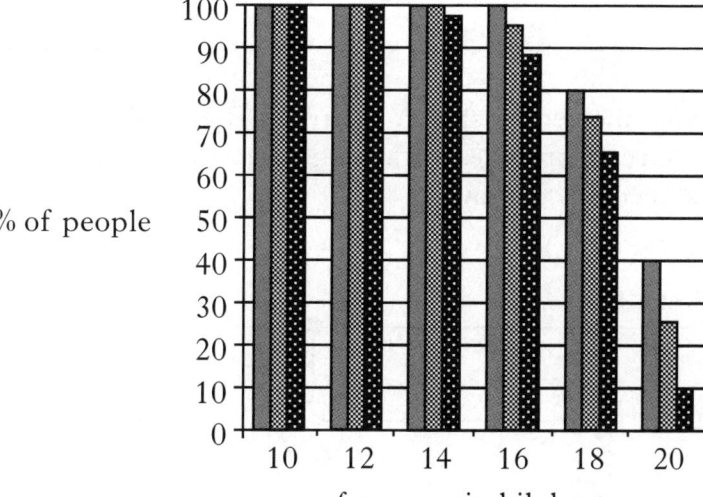

% of people

frequency in kilohertz

■ 15–20 yrs
▨ 35–40 yrs
▩ 55–60 yrs

(i) State **two** conclusions which can be made from this bar graph about the hearing of different age groups.

....

.... **2**

(ii) What name is given to sound frequencies greater than 20 kilohertz?

.... **1**

Marks

11. (*a*) A thermistor is connected to a 6·0 volt supply in circuit 1. The table gives some information about the thermistor.

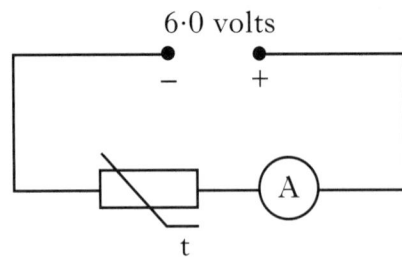

6·0 volts

circuit 1

temperature (degrees Celsius)	resistance (ohms)
20	1000
30	600
40	400

Calculate the reading on the ammeter when the thermistor is placed in a beaker of water at 40 degrees celsius.

Space for working and answer

3

(*b*) The thermistor is now connected as shown in circuit 2 and placed in a tropical fish tank. The circuit provides a warning when the temperature of the water in the tank becomes too low.

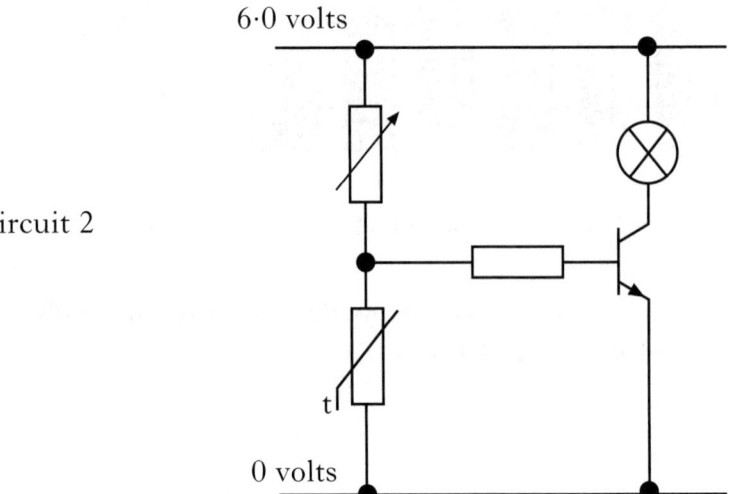

6·0 volts

circuit 2

0 volts

(i) What is the purpose of the transistor in circuit 2?

....   1

K&U	PS

Marks

11. **(b)** **(continued)**

(ii) The same components are used to construct circuit 3.

circuit 3

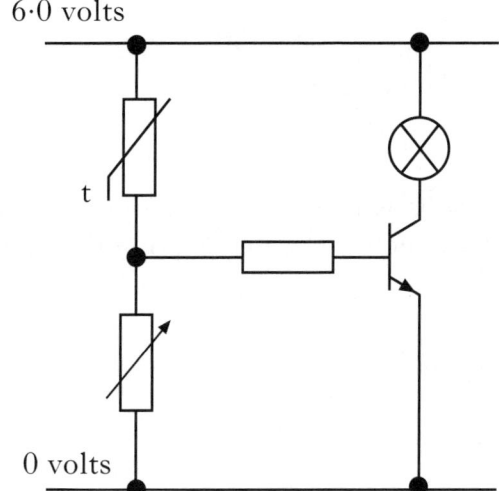

6·0 volts

0 volts

State how the operation of circuit 3 differs from the operation of circuit 2.

.... **1**

[Turn over

K&U

Marks

12. (*a*) A nurse uses a clinical thermometer to measure the body temperature of a patient. The temperature of the patient is 39 degrees celsius.

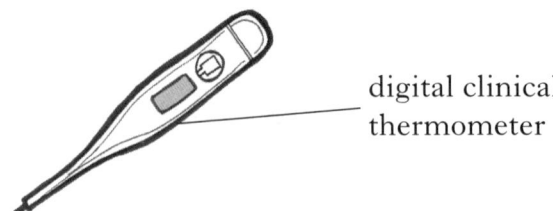

digital clinical
thermometer

(i) Give **two** reasons why a clinical thermometer is used instead of an ordinary thermometer when measuring the body temperature of the patient.

....

....   **2**

(ii) Why does the nurse conclude that the patient is unwell?

....   **1**

(*b*) Radioactive sources are used in the treatment of many illnesses. The table below gives some properties of three radioactive sources used in medicine.

Name of Source	Type of Source	Half-life of Source
Radium – 226	Alpha	1600 years
Iodine – 131	Beta	8 days
Technetium – 99	Gamma	6 hours

(i) One type of treatment requires a source that produces high ionisation.
Which source should be used?

....   **1**

(ii) Which source would be most suitable for use in diagnostic tests where a tracer is injected into the body?

....   **1**

(iii) Which source should not be stored in an aluminium box for safety reasons?

....   **1**

13. An electronic system is designed to count the number of vehicles that enter a car park.

When a vehicle enters the car park it cuts through a beam of light and a sensor circuit produces a digital pulse. The number of pulses produced by the sensor circuit is then counted and decoded before being displayed. The display consists of a number of illuminated sections.

A diagram for part of this system is shown.

(a) (i) Select a suitable device **from the list below** to be used as an input for the sensor circuit.

LDR   **thermistor**   **microphone**   **capacitor**

.... 1

(ii) Complete the sentence below by circling the correct answer.

The output of the counter is $\begin{Bmatrix} \text{analogue} \\ \text{binary} \\ \text{decimal} \end{Bmatrix}$. 1

(iii) Name the device used to display the number of vehicles that enter the car park.

.... 1

(b) The counter is reset to zero. Over a period of time, the sensor circuit then produces the following signal.

logic level 1

logic level 0

On the diagram of the display below, shade in the sections that should be illuminated to show the number of vehicles that have entered the car park during this time.

1

Marks

14. A walker wears a pedometer. A pedometer is an instrument that measures the distance walked by counting the number of steps taken. The walker measures the distance of one step as 0·8 metres, and enters it into the pedometer.

0·8 metres

(*a*) The walker completes 9000 steps during a walk.

Calculate the distance travelled.

> *Space for working and answer*

1

(*b*) The walker completes this walk in 80 minutes.

What is the average speed of the walker in **metres per second**?

> *Space for working and answer*

2

(*c*) Give a reason why the distance measured by the pedometer may not be accurate.

.... 1

Marks

15. A piano of mass 250 kilograms is pushed up a ramp into a van by applying a constant force of 600 newtons as shown.

The ramp is 3 metres long and the van floor is 0·75 metres above the ground.

piano

600 N

(*a*) (i) Calculate the weight of the piano.

> *Space for working and answer*

2

    (ii) What is the minimum force required to lift the piano vertically into the van?

.... **1**

(*b*) Calculate the work done pushing the piano up the ramp.

> *Space for working and answer*

2

(*c*) How can the force required to push the piano up the ramp be reduced?

.... **1**

[Turn over

Marks

16. A traffic information sign is located in a remote area.

The sign is supplied with energy by both a panel of solar cells and a wind generator. The panel of solar cells and the wind generator are connected to a rechargeable battery.

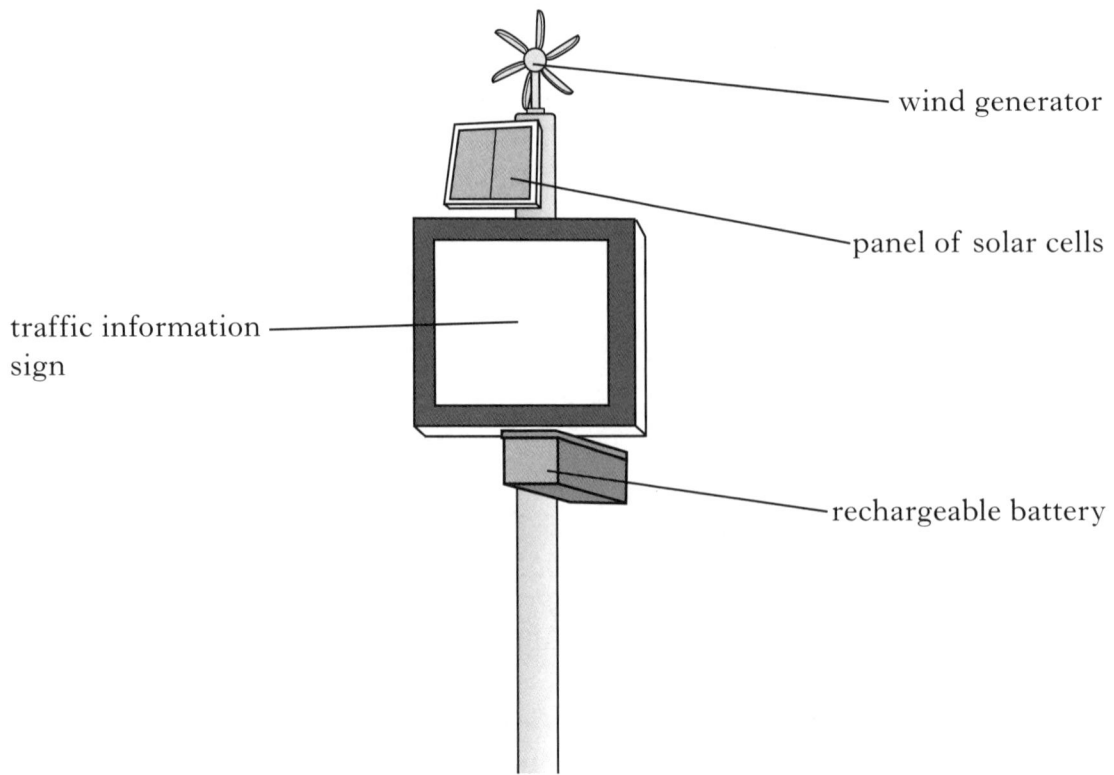

(*a*) One square metre of solar cells can generate up to 80 watts.

The panel of solar cells has an area of 0·4 square metres.

(i) State the energy change that takes place in the solar cells.

....   **1**

(ii) Calculate the maximum power produced by the panel of solar cells.

Space for working and answer

1

16. (continued)

(b) The following table shows the power produced by the wind generator at different wind speeds.

wind speed (metres per second)	power output of wind generator (watts)
2	8
4	16
6	
8	32
10	40

(i) Suggest the power produced when the wind speed is 6 metres per second.

....   1

(ii) At a wind speed of 10 metres per second the voltage produced by the wind generator is 16 volts.

Calculate the current produced by the wind generator.

Space for working and answer

2

(c) Explain why a rechargeable battery is also required to supply energy to the traffic information sign.

....   1

[Turn over

Marks

17. (*a*) A digital camera contains a rechargeable battery. The battery requires a voltage of 5·75 volts to be recharged. The battery is recharged using a transformer connected to the mains supply. The transformer is used to step down the 230 volt a.c. mains supply to 5·75 volts.

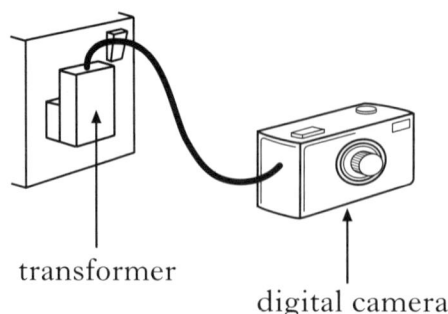

transformer

digital camera

The transformer has 2000 turns on the primary coil.

(i) Calculate the number of turns on the secondary coil.

Space for working and answer

2

(ii) Give **one** reason why a transformer cannot be used to charge the camera battery from a 12 volt d.c. car battery.

.... **1**

(*b*) Complete the following passage.

In the National Grid, ... transformers are used to increase the 25 000 volts from a power station to 132 000 volts for transmission.

This reduces .... in the transmission lines.

The voltage is then decreased to 11 000 volts for industry and 230 volts

for domestic use using .... transformers. **3**

18. A coolant pack is used to treat an injured player at a hockey match.

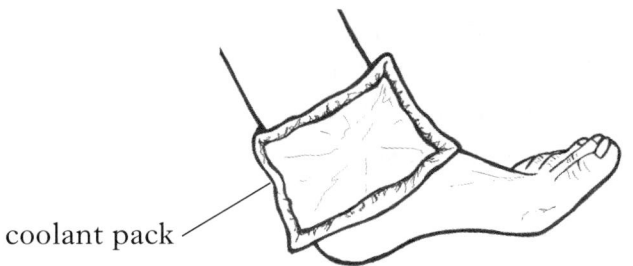

coolant pack

Before use the coolant pack is stored in a refrigerator at 2 degrees celsius.

The coolant inside the pack changes state from liquid to solid.

The coolant has a melting point of 7 degrees celsius and a mass of 0·5 kilograms.

The coolant pack is removed from the refrigerator and placed on the injured ankle of a player.

(a) (i) Calculate the energy required to raise the temperature of the coolant pack from 2 degrees celsius to its melting point.

(specific heat capacity of coolant = 2100 joules per kilogram per degree celsius)

> *Space for working and answer*

3

(ii) Where does most of the energy required to raise the temperature of the coolant pack come from?

.... **1**

(b) Having reached its melting point the coolant pack then remains at the same temperature for 15 minutes.

What is happening to the coolant during this time?

.... **1**

(c) One of the other players suggests insulating the coolant pack and ankle with a towel.

Why should this be done?

.... **1**

Marks

19. Read the following passage about a space mission to the moons of Jupiter.

The spacecraft will use a new kind of engine called an ion drive. The ion drive will propel the spacecraft away from Earth on its journey to the moons of Jupiter, although for much of the journey the engine will be switched off.

The spacecraft will first visit the moon Callisto.

Callisto is only slightly smaller than the planet Mercury. Next, the spacecraft will visit Ganymede, the largest moon in the Solar System, before travelling on to Europa.

The radiation around Europa is so intense that the spacecraft will not be able to operate for long before becoming damaged beyond repair.

The spacecraft will eventually burn up in the atmosphere of Jupiter.

(a) (i) Name one object, **mentioned in the passage**, which orbits a planet.

.... 1

(ii) State what is meant by the term Solar System.

.... 1

(b) (i) The ion drive engine exerts a backward force on small particles called ions.

Explain how the ion drive engine is propelled forwards.

.... 1

(ii) The mass of the spacecraft is 1200 kilograms and the thrust produced by the engine is 3 newtons.

Calculate the maximum acceleration produced by the ion drive engine.

Space for working and answer

2

(c) State why the ion drive engine need not be kept on for most of the journey from Earth to Jupiter.

.... 1

20. (*a*) A ray of green light strikes a triangular prism as shown.

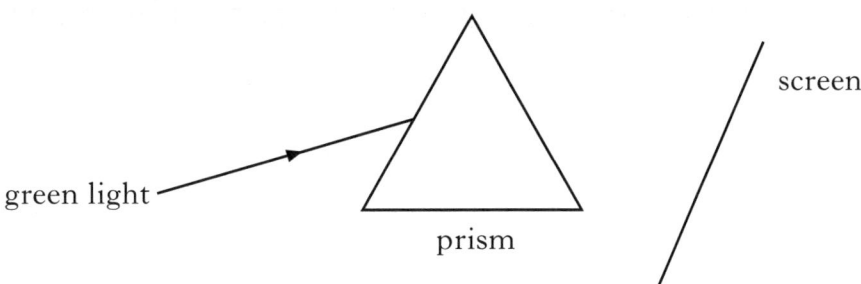

(i) Complete the diagram to show the path of the ray of green light as it passes through the prism and on to the screen.

1

(ii) The green light is now replaced by white light.
Describe what is now observed on the screen.

....

1

(iii) State **one** colour which has a longer wavelength than green light.

....

1

(*b*) Light from a star produces a line spectrum.
What information is obtained about the star from this spectrum?

....

1

[END OF QUESTION PAPER]

YOU MAY USE THE SPACE ON THIS PAGE TO REWRITE ANY ANSWER YOU HAVE DECIDED TO CHANGE IN THE MAIN PART OF THE ANSWER BOOKLET. TAKE CARE TO WRITE IN CAREFULLY THE APPROPRIATE QUESTION NUMBER.

K&U	PS

YOU MAY USE THE SPACE ON THIS PAGE TO REWRITE ANY ANSWER YOU HAVE DECIDED TO CHANGE IN THE MAIN PART OF THE ANSWER BOOKLET. TAKE CARE TO WRITE IN CAREFULLY THE APPROPRIATE QUESTION NUMBER.

DO N
WRIT
TH
MARC

K&U

YOU MAY USE THE SPACE ON THIS PAGE TO REWRITE ANY ANSWER YOU HAVE DECIDED TO CHANGE IN THE MAIN PART OF THE ANSWER BOOKLET. TAKE CARE TO WRITE IN CAREFULLY THE APPROPRIATE QUESTION NUMBER.

DO NOT
WRITE IN
THIS
MARGIN

K&U | PS

YOU MAY USE THE SPACE ON THIS PAGE TO REWRITE ANY ANSWER YOU HAVE DECIDED TO CHANGE IN THE MAIN PART OF THE ANSWER BOOKLET. TAKE CARE TO WRITE IN CAREFULLY THE APPROPRIATE QUESTION NUMBER.

[BLANK PAGE]

STANDARD GRADE | GENERAL

2009

[BLANK PAGE]

FOR OFFICIAL USE

K&U   PS

G

3220/401

NATIONAL
QUALIFICATIONS
2009

TUESDAY, 26 MAY
9.00 AM – 10.30 AM

PHYSICS
STANDARD GRADE
General Level

Fill in these boxes and read what is printed below.

Full name of centre

Town

Forename(s)

Surname

Date of birth
Day   Month   Year

Scottish candidate number

Number of seat

Reference may be made to the Physics Data Booklet.

1 All questions should be answered.

2 The questions may be answered in any order but all answers must be written clearly and legibly in this book.

3 For questions 1–6, write down, in the space provided, the letter corresponding to the answer you think is correct. There is only **one** correct answer.

4 For questions 7–20, write your answer where indicated by the question or in the space provided after the question.

5 If you change your mind about your answer you may score it out and replace it in the space provided at the end of the answer book.

6 If you use the additional space at the end of the answer book for answering any questions, you **must** write the correct question number beside each answer.

7 Before leaving the examination room you must give this book to the invigilator. If you do not, you may lose all the marks for this paper.

Use **blue** or **black ink**. Pencil may be used for graphs and diagrams only.

Marks

1. What is the frequency of a wave, if 20 crests pass a point in two seconds?

    A   0·1 hertz

    B   2   hertz

    C   10   hertz

    D   20   hertz

    E   40   hertz

    Answer ☐   1

2. How long does a geostationary satellite take to orbit the Earth?

    A   1 hour

    B   1 day

    C   1 week

    D   1 month

    E   1 year

    Answer ☐   1

3. Which of the following will **not allow** the transmission of sound waves?

    A   Brick

    B   Vacuum

    C   Water

    D   Air

    E   Wood

    Answer ☐   1

4. Which of the following statements is **always** true about the structure of the atom?

    A   It has more electrons than protons.

    B   It has more protons than neutrons.

    C   It has an equal number of protons and electrons.

    D   It has more neutrons than protons.

    E   It has an equal number of neutrons and electrons.

    Answer ☐   1

5. Which of the following is a digital output device?

    A   Solenoid

    B   Loudspeaker

    C   Motor

    D   Lamp

    E   Microphone

                                            Answer ☐   **1**

6. In which of the following would a voltage **not** be induced in a coil of wire?

    A   Rotating the coil of wire near to a magnet

    B   Rotating a magnet near to the coil of wire

    C   Holding a magnet stationary within the coil of wire

    D   Moving a magnet in and out of the coil of wire

    E   Moving the coil of wire between the poles of a magnet

                                            Answer ☐   **1**

[Turn over

Marks

7. A student listens to his radio using headphones.

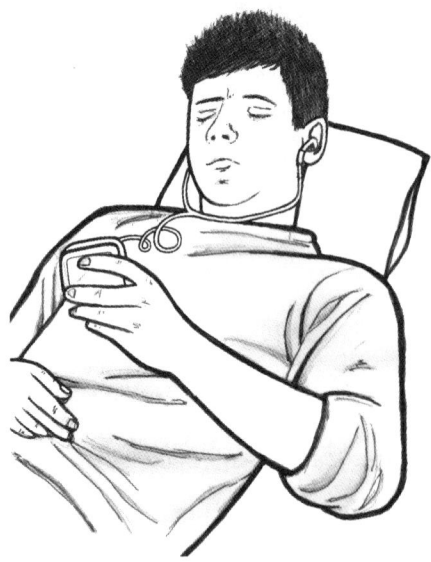

(a) State the main energy transformation that takes place in the headphones.

....   **1**

The table shows the frequencies for different radio stations.

Radio Station	Frequency (mega hertz)
Forth 1	97·3
Real Radio	101·0
Radio Borders	103·1
Isles	103·0
Central Scotland FM	103·1
Radio Scotland	95·0

(b) Explain why the radio stations Radio Borders and Central Scotland FM are allowed to transmit at the same frequency.

....   **1**

Marks

7.   **(continued)**

(*c*) The block diagram shows some of the main parts of a radio receiver.

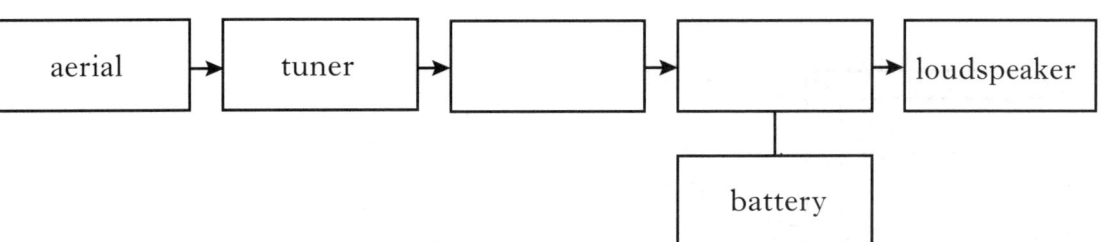

(i)   Complete the block diagram by filling in the missing labels.   **1**

(ii) What is the purpose of the tuner?

....   **1**

[Turn over

Marks

8. An experiment is set up to investigate sound waves.

A signal generator is connected to a loudspeaker.

The signal generator has a frequency control and an amplitude control.

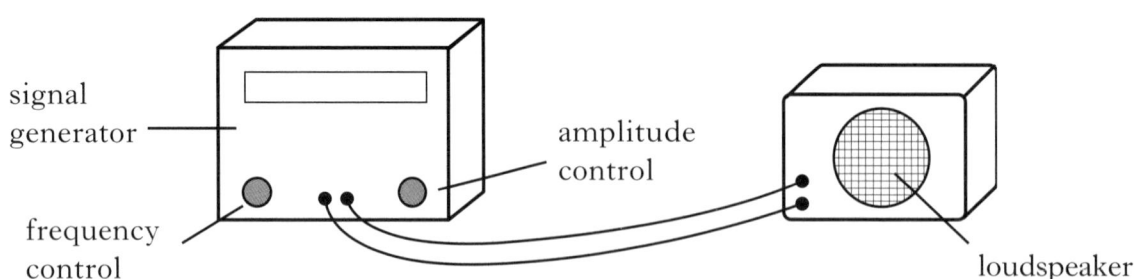

(*a*) Complete the sentence below by circling the correct answer.

The $\left\{ \begin{array}{c} \text{amplitude} \\ \text{frequency} \end{array} \right\}$ control is used to adjust the loudness of the sound wave.   **1**

(*b*) The controls of the signal generator are set up to produce a sound wave from the loudspeaker.

An oscilloscope is now connected across the loudspeaker.

The oscilloscope trace is shown in Figure 1.

Complete Figure 2 to show the trace obtained when the frequency is **doubled**, but the amplitude remains unchanged.

The oscilloscope controls are unchanged.

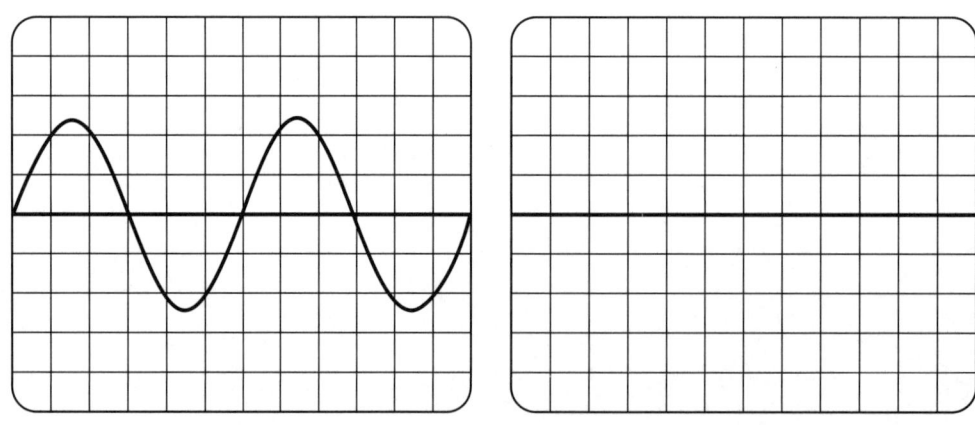

Figure 1   Figure 2   **2**

Marks

9. A design engineer uses three ammeters to measure the current, in amperes, at various points in the circuit of a model-sized electrical fan heater.

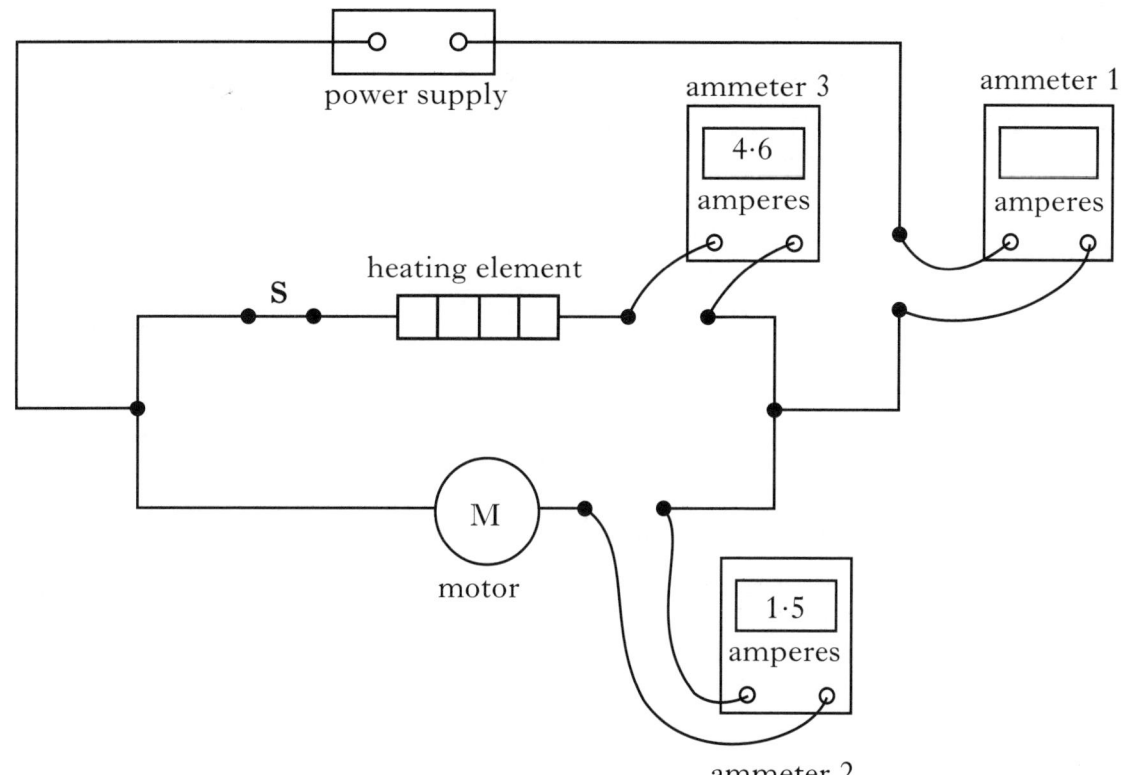

(a) Calculate the reading on ammeter 1.

Space for working and answer

1

(b) What happens to the reading on ammeter 1 when switch **S** is opened?

.... 1

(c) The full size mains fan heater has a rating plate for UK supply stating its operating voltage and frequency.

Complete parts (i) and (ii) below by circling the correct answers.

(i) The voltage is $\begin{Bmatrix} 110 \\ 230 \\ 325 \end{Bmatrix}$ volts $\begin{Bmatrix} \text{a.c.} \\ \text{d.c.} \end{Bmatrix}$. 2

(ii) The mains frequency is $\begin{Bmatrix} 50 \\ 60 \\ 115 \end{Bmatrix}$ hertz. 1

DO NO
WRITE
THIS
MARG

K&U   I

Marks

10. Party lights consist of 16 identical light bulbs connected in series.

They operate from a 24 volt power supply. The current in the circuit is 1·25 amperes.

(*a*) Calculate the total resistance of the bulbs in the circuit.

> *Space for working and answer*

2

(*b*) Calculate the voltage across each light bulb.

> *Space for working and answer*

1

(*c*) A fault occurs in the circuit and a continuity tester is needed to find the fault. The circuit diagram for the continuity tester is shown.

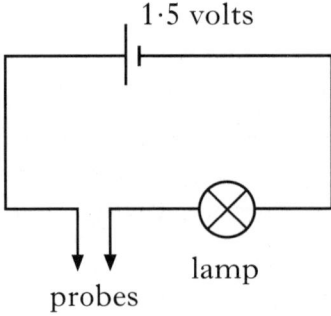

1·5 volts

lamp

probes

(i) Describe how the continuity tester could be tested to make sure that it is working.

.... 1

(ii) The continuity tester is found to be faulty.

State one possible reason why it is not working.

.... 1

10. (continued)

(*d*) Conventional filament lamps are now being replaced by discharge tubes.

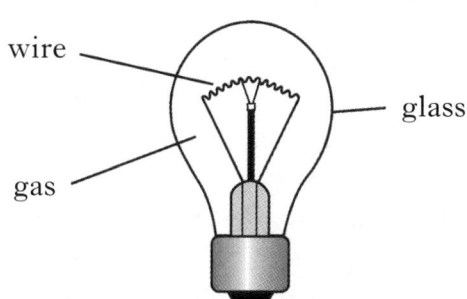

filament lamp

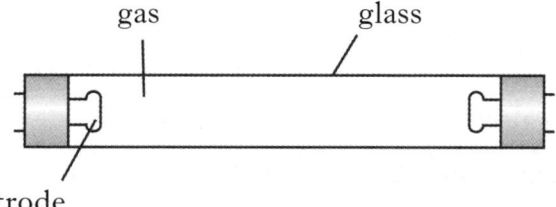

discharge tube

(i) State where the energy transformation occurs in:

(A) the filament lamp;

.... **1**

(B) the discharge tube.

.... **1**

(ii) State why discharge tubes are replacing conventional filament lamps.

.... **1**

[Turn over

DO NOT
WRITE
THIS
MARG

K&U

Marks

11. The electromagnetic spectrum is shown below.

radio & tv	microwaves	infrared	visible light	ultraviolet	X-rays	gamma rays

electromagnetic spectrum

Different types of waves in the spectrum are used in medicine.

(*a*) What property do all electromagnetic waves have in common?

.... 1

(*b*) Describe **one** use of X-rays in medicine.

.... 1

(*c*) Gamma radiation is used in medicine as a tracer.

A tracer is a radioactive substance injected into the body.

The gamma radiation then given off from the body is monitored.

(i) Explain why gamma radiation is used rather than alpha or beta radiation.

....

.... 1

(ii) What is the unit for the activity of the gamma radiation?

.... 1

(*d*) Light can be produced by lasers.

Describe the use of the laser in **one** application of medicine.

....

.... 1

Marks

11.   (continued)

(e)   A student sets up the following experiment to compare how two different brands of sunglasses protect from ultraviolet radiation.

The student uses beads which change colour when exposed to ultraviolet radiation.

The student covers one set of beads with a lens from brand A and another with a lens from brand B.

The ultraviolet lamp is switched on for 30 minutes.

The apparatus is set up as shown.

ultraviolet lamp

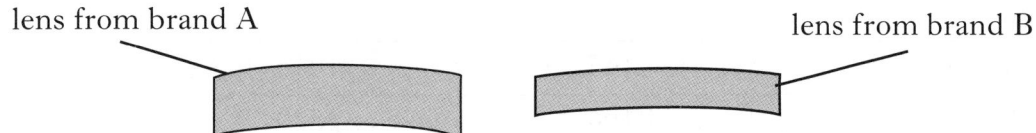
lens from brand A

lens from brand B

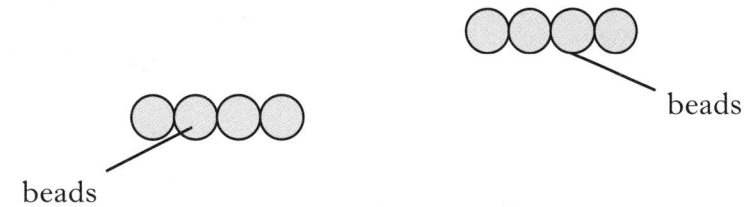
beads

beads

(i)   Give **one** reason why this test is not a fair one.

....   1

(ii)   Why can exposure to ultraviolet radiation be harmful to humans?

....   1

[Turn over

Marks

12. An orchestra uses many different musical instruments.

The table lists the lowest and highest sound frequencies for some of these instruments.

Musical Instrument	Lowest Frequency (hertz)	Highest Frequency (hertz)
Acoustic Guitar	73	1174
Piano	28	4186
Flute	261	2637
Trumpet	165	1046
Violin	196	3520
Cello	65	660
Piccolo	523	4000

(*a*) (i) Which instrument in the table produces the longest wavelength?

.... **1**

(ii) Calculate the wavelength for the lowest frequency of a piccolo.

(The speed of sound in air is 340 metres per second.)

Space for working and answer

2

(*b*) During one concert performance the sound level was measured.

State the unit of sound level measurement.

.... **1**

Marks

13. A radio controlled model fire engine receives signals from a control unit.

One of the control functions operates a siren on the fire engine.

(a) State a suitable output device for the siren.

.... **1**

(b) The fire engine contains an electronic system to control the siren.

The signals at various parts of the system are displayed on oscilloscope screens.

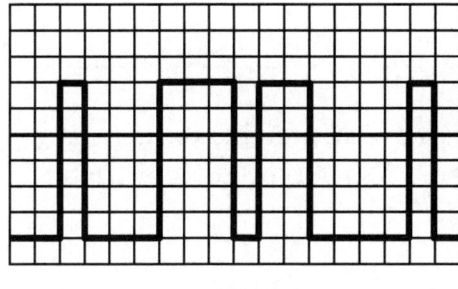

screen 1

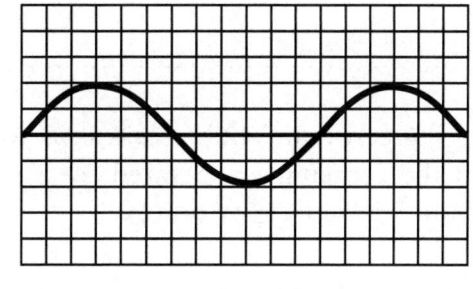

screen 2

(i) Which screen shows a digital signal?

.... **1**

(ii) The signal shown on screen 2 is now amplified.

The oscilloscope settings are unchanged.

Draw the amplified signal in the box below.

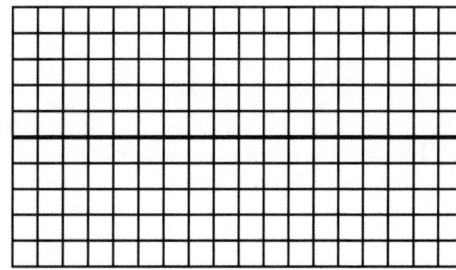

2

Marks

14. A pedestrian crossing at a set of traffic lights has an electronic control system to operate the "green man" light. Part of the system is shown.

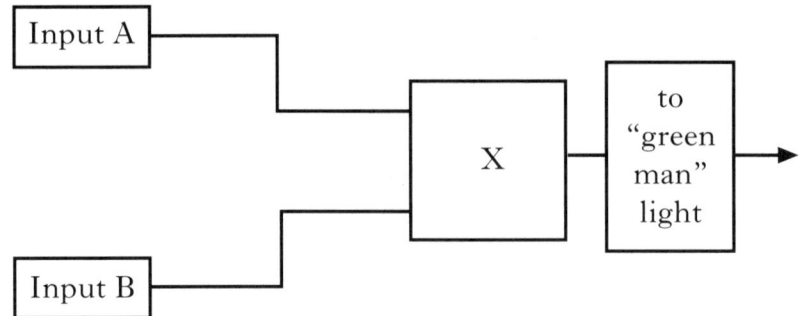

Input A is from the traffic lights and gives a logic 1 when the red light only is on, and a logic 0 at other times.

Input B is operated by pedestrians when they want to cross.

(a) State a suitable input device to be used by the pedestrians to activate the "green man" light.

.... 1

(b) The "green man" light comes on when the red traffic light, only, is on and the crossing is operated by a pedestrian. What type of logic gate should be used at position X?

.... 1

(c) The "green man" light consists of a number of LEDs.

(i) Draw the symbol for an LED.

Space for symbol

1

(ii) Why does each LED need a series resistor?

.... 1

DO NOT WRITE IN THIS MARGIN

K&U	PS

Marks

14. (continued)

(*d*) The "green man" light has to stay on long enough for the pedestrian to cross.

This crossing has a display to show pedestrians the number of seconds the "green man" light will remain on.

State an output device that could be used to display this time.

.... **1**

[Turn over

DO NOT
WRITE
THIS
MARGIN

K&U F

Marks

15. An indoor kart track hosts a racing competition.

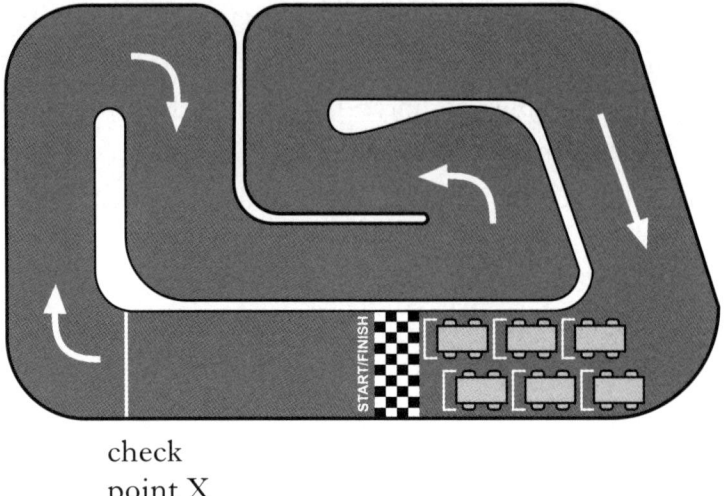

check
point X

(*a*) Describe how to find the average speed of a kart for one complete lap of the track.

You must state the measurements that are made and how they are used.

....

....

.... **3**

(*b*) The speed of a kart and driver is recorded from the start of the race.

The kart starts from rest and accelerates uniformly until it reaches check point X. Its speed at X is 12 metres per second.

The time taken to reach X is 4 seconds.

(i) Draw a speed-time graph for the motion of the kart from the start until it reaches check point X.

Units and numerical values must be shown on both axes.

speed in

....

....

....

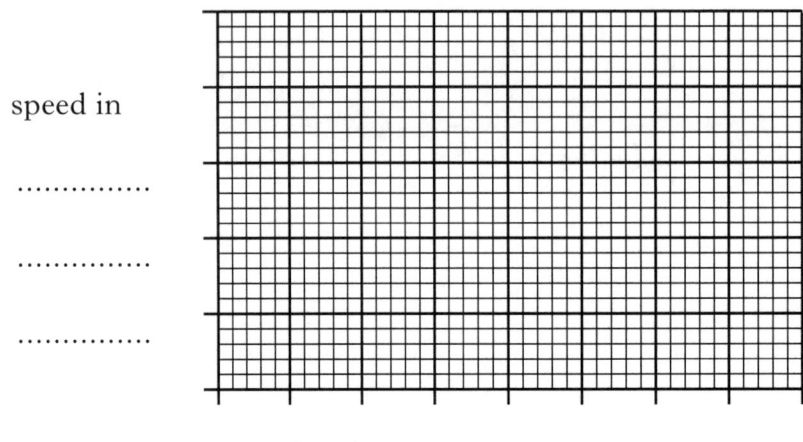

time in **3**

Marks

15. (*b*) **(continued)**

(ii) Calculate the acceleration of the kart between the start and check point X.

Space for working and answer

2

(*c*) Some spectators at the race track are finding it difficult to see the race.

One spectator uses a periscope. A periscope can be made from a cardboard tube with two plane mirrors as shown.

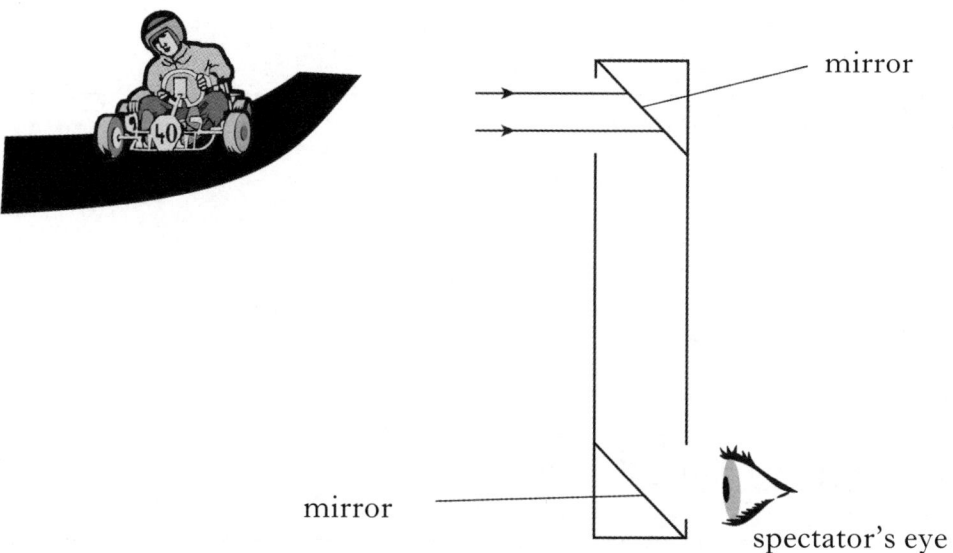

mirror

mirror

spectator's eye

Complete the diagram to show how the rays of light travel through the periscope to the spectator's eye.

1

[Turn over

Marks

16. A climber of weight 550 newtons takes 40 seconds to reach the top of a 20 metre high climbing wall.

(a) What is the minimum upward force she exerts while climbing the wall?

.... **1**

(b) Calculate the minimum work done by the climber to reach the top of the wall.

Space for working and answer

2

(c) Calculate her power during this climb.

Space for working and answer

2

(d) Explain why the climber uses chalk on her hands as she climbs the wall.

.... **1**

Marks

17. A house is designed to conserve as much energy as possible.

(*a*) Heat energy can be lost from the house by a variety of means. Insulation is used to reduce heat loss.

Match the correct type of insulation given in the word bank with each type of heat loss.

Use each answer once only.

foil-backed plasterboard	double glazing	loft insulation

Type of heat loss	Correct insulation
Conduction	
Convection	
Radiation	

2

The temperature in the house is kept at a constant value while the temperature outside changes.

The graph shows the temperature inside the house and the temperature outside the house over a 24 hour period.

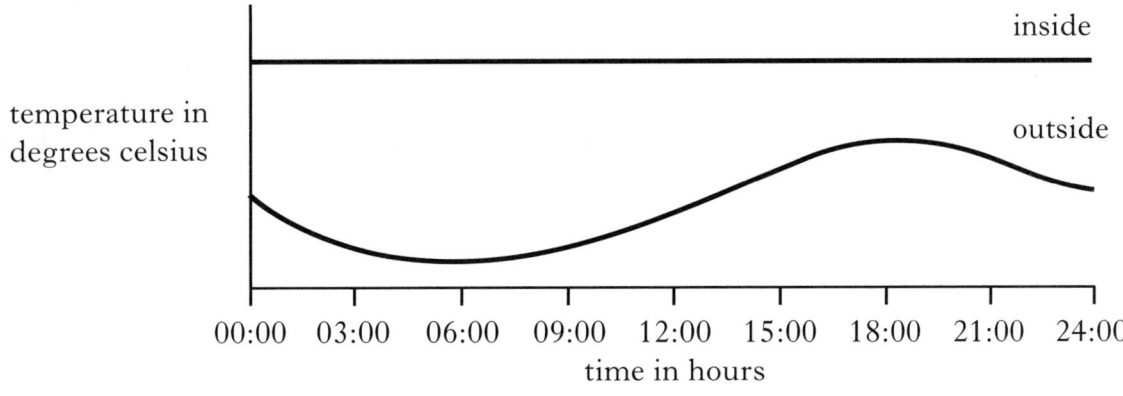

(*b*) Write down the time at which heat loss from the house is greatest.

.... 1

K&U

Marks

18. Increasing the amount of electricity generated from renewable sources is important for the future of our country.

(*a*) At present, fossil fuels are the main source of energy.

State **one** problem with this source of energy.

.... **1**

(*b*) The bar chart shows the main energy sources used in Scotland.

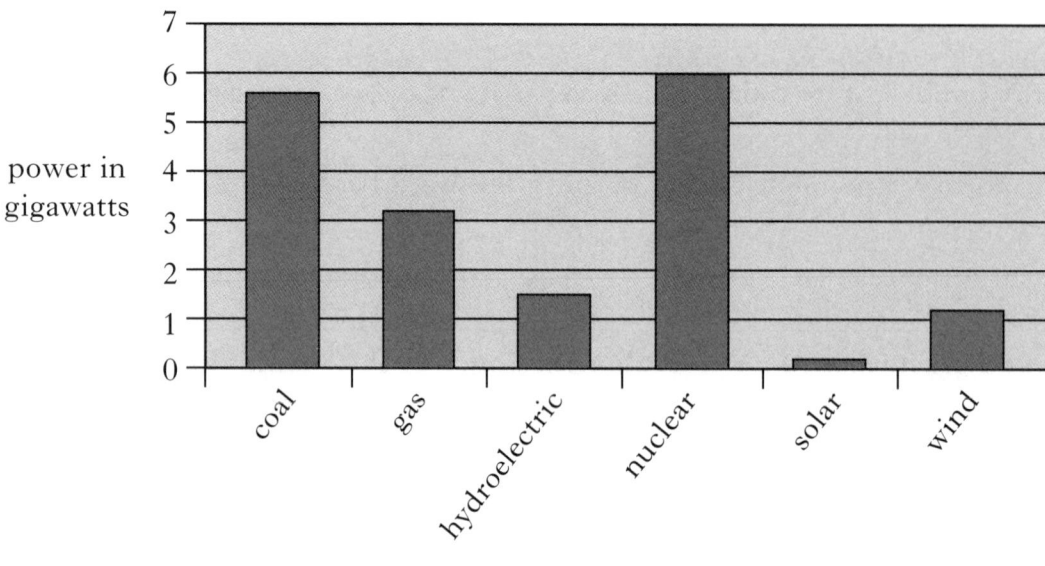

energy sources

Use the names of the energy sources in the bar chart to complete the table.

Renewable	*Non-renewable*

2

Marks

K&U PS

18. **(continued)**

(c) A nuclear power station with a power output of 1·5 gigawatts could be replaced by pumped hydroelectric power stations.

(i) Some of the stages in a nuclear power station are shown.

| Reactor | → | Turbine | → | Generator | → | National Grid |

At what stage is the main energy transformation:

(A) kinetic → electrical;

.... 1

(B) nuclear → heat?

.... 1

A pumped hydroelectric power station produces 0·25 gigawatts of power.

(ii) Give **one** advantage of a pumped hydroelectric station over a normal hydroelectric station.

....

.... 1

(iii) How many pumped hydroelectric stations would be needed to replace the nuclear power station?

Space for working and answer

1

[Turn over

Marks

19. (*a*) State an optical device that can split white light into different colours.

.... 1

(*b*) Astronomers can use the peak wavelength of light emitted by stars to provide information about their temperature. The peak wavelength corresponds to a particular colour.

Information about three stars is given in the table.

Star	Colour of peak wavelength in visible spectrum
Rigel	Blue
Betelgeuse	Red
Sun	Green

The shorter the peak wavelength, the hotter the star is.

(i) Which star is hottest?

.... 1

(ii) Is the sun hotter, colder or the same temperature as Betelgeuse?

.... 1

(*c*) Telescopes can detect visible light waves.

Name **one** other type of wave that can be detected using a telescope.

.... 1

Marks

19. (continued)

(d) The planet Venus is often seen in the evening and morning close to the horizon.

Draw light rays on the diagram to show how observers on Earth are able to see Venus.

You must put arrows on the rays to show their direction.

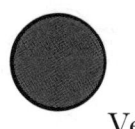

Venus

Earth

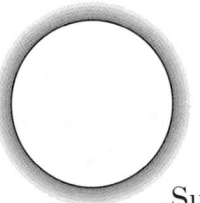

Sun

2

[Turn over

K&U F

Marks

20. Astronomers study space.

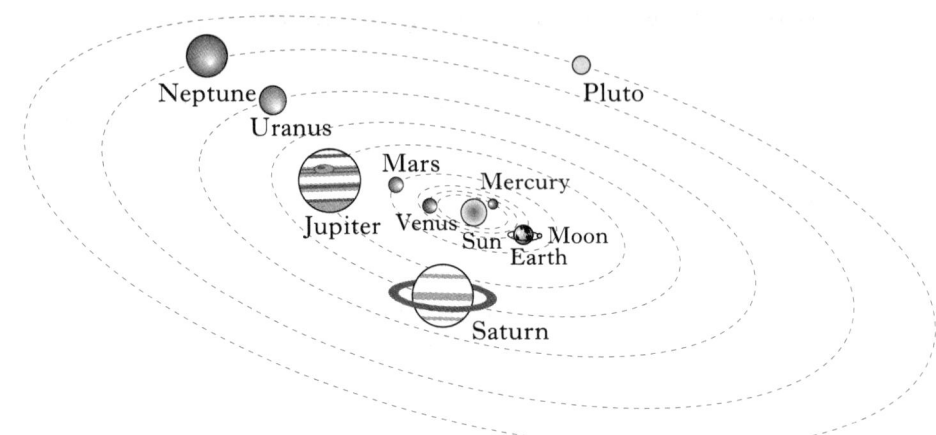

Complete the sentences by circling the correct answers.

(a) The Earth is a $\begin{Bmatrix} \text{planet} \\ \text{moon} \\ \text{star} \end{Bmatrix}$ which orbits the Sun. The Earth has one natural

satellite called the $\begin{Bmatrix} \text{International Space station} \\ \text{Hubble telescope} \\ \text{Moon} \end{Bmatrix}$.   **1**

(b) The Sun is at the centre of our $\begin{Bmatrix} \text{solar system} \\ \text{universe} \\ \text{galaxy} \end{Bmatrix}$. Light from the Sun takes

about $\begin{Bmatrix} \text{8 seconds} \\ \text{4·3 years} \\ \text{8 minutes} \end{Bmatrix}$ to travel to the Earth.   **1**

(c) The nearest star to the Earth is $\begin{Bmatrix} \text{Sirius} \\ \text{Mars} \\ \text{the Sun} \end{Bmatrix}$.

All of space is known as the $\begin{Bmatrix} \text{Milky Way} \\ \text{solar system} \\ \text{universe} \end{Bmatrix}$.   **1**

[END OF QUESTION PAPER]

ADDITIONAL SPACE FOR ANSWERS

Make sure you write the correct question number beside each answer.

ADDITIONAL SPACE FOR ANSWERS

Make sure you write the correct question number beside each answer.

ADDITIONAL SPACE FOR ANSWERS

Make sure you write the correct question number beside each answer.

ADDITIONAL SPACE FOR ANSWERS

Make sure you write the correct question number beside each answer.

[BLANK PAGE]

FOR OFFICIAL USE

K&U   PS

3220/401

G

NATIONAL
QUALIFICATIONS
2010

FRIDAY, 28 MAY
9.00 AM – 10.30 AM

PHYSICS
STANDARD GRADE
General Level

Fill in these boxes and read what is printed below.

Full name of centre

Town

Forename(s)

Surname

Date of birth

Day   Month   Year

Scottish candidate number

Number of seat

Reference may be made to the Physics Data Booklet.

1 All questions should be answered.

2 The questions may be answered in any order but all answers must be written clearly and legibly in this book.

3 For questions 1–5, write down, in the space provided, the letter corresponding to the answer you think is correct. There is only **one** correct answer.

4 For questions 6–19, write your answer where indicated by the question or in the space provided after the question.

5 If you change your mind about your answer you may score it out and replace it in the space provided at the end of the answer book.

6 If you use the additional space at the end of the answer book for answering any questions, you **must** write the correct question number beside each answer.

7 Before leaving the examination room you must give this book to the Invigilator. If you do not, you may lose all the marks for this paper .

Use **blue** or **black ink**. Pencil may be used for graphs and diagrams only.

[BLANK PAGE]

1. Optical fibres used in telecommunication systems are made from

   A   copper

   B   cotton

   C   water

   D   glass

   E   aluminium.

   Answer ☐   **1**

2. The three colours of light that mix to produce all the colours seen on a TV screen are

   A   red, green and blue

   B   red, yellow and blue

   C   magenta, green and cyan

   D   magenta, yellow and cyan

   E   green, yellow and blue.

   Answer ☐   **1**

[Turn over

Marks K&U P

3. Which of the following diagrams shows the correct path of a ray of blue light as it passes from air into a glass prism?

A

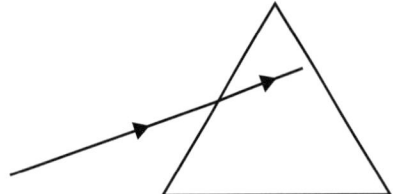

B

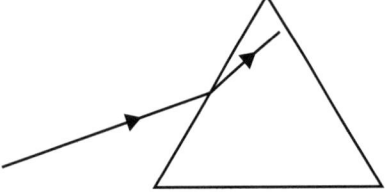

C

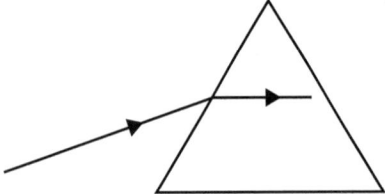

D

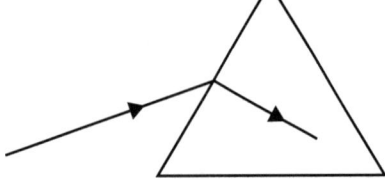

E

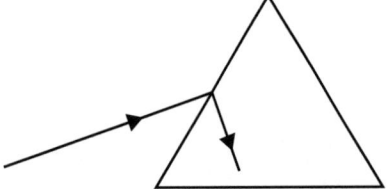

Answer ☐   **1**

Marks | K&U | PS

4. A stethoscope is used to

A   measure body temperature

B   correct long sight

C   treat skin diseases

D   listen to sounds within the body

E   produce an image of the inside of the body.

Answer ☐   **1**

5. Which one of the following sources of energy is renewable?

A   uranium

B   hydroelectric

C   coal

D   oil

E   gas

Answer ☐   **1**

[Turn over

Marks K&U P

6. The diagram shows part of a water tank used to test a model wave power generator.

model wave power generator

A wave power generator uses waves to generate electricity.

(*a*) (i) A machine in the tank produces 20 waves in 10 seconds.

Calculate the frequency of the waves.

> *Space for working and answer*

1

(ii) The wavelength of the waves in the tank is 1·2 metres.

Calculate the speed of the waves in the tank.

> *Space for working and answer*

2

(*b*) The amplitude of the waves in the tank is 0·15 metres.

Calculate the maximum vertical distance the wave power generator moves through.

> *Space for working and answer*

1

7. A satellite navigation system receives radio signals transmitted by satellites in orbit around the Earth.

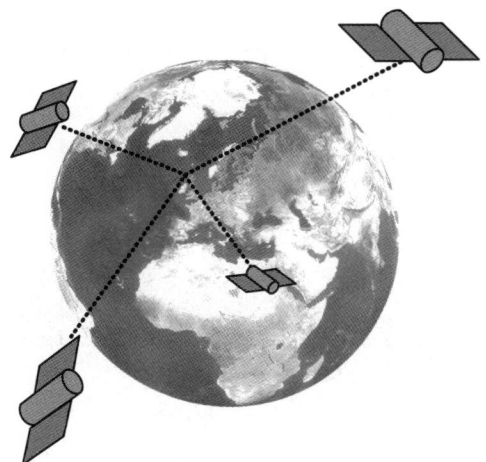

The satellite navigation system finds its location by calculating the distance the transmitted signals travel.

(a) In addition to the speed of the signals, what other quantity must be known to calculate distance?

.... **1**

(b) Complete the passage below using words from the following list.

greater   sound   light   energy   height   mass   less

Radio signals are waves which transfer .... The

radio signals travel at the speed of light, which is ....

than the speed of sound. The period of a satellite orbit depends on its

.... above the Earth. **3**

(c) A curved reflector is often used to make the signals received from a satellite stronger. Complete the diagram to show the effect of a curved reflector on the transmitted signals.

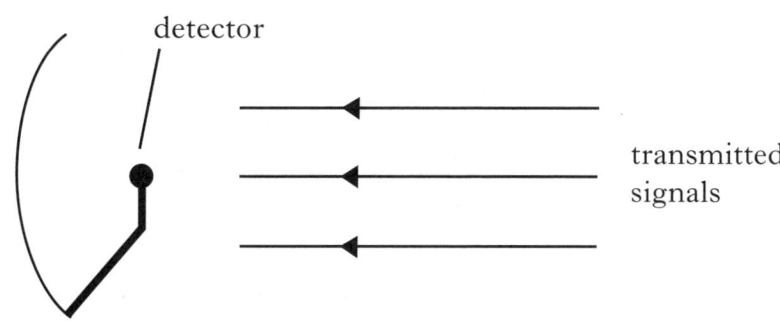

detector

transmitted signals

2

Marks K&U P

8. (*a*) Three **identical** lamps are connected as shown in circuit 1. A 12·0 volt battery supplies a current of 0·2 ampere.

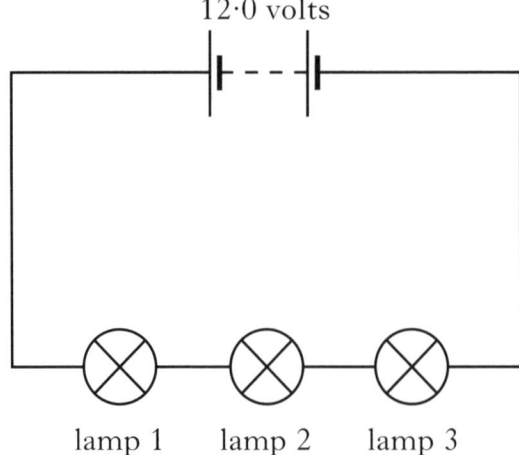

12·0 volts

lamp 1   lamp 2   lamp 3

Circuit 1

(i) State the current in lamp 2.

.... **1**

(ii) Calculate the voltage across lamp 2.

Space for working and answer

1

Marks | K&U | PS

8. (continued)

(b) The lamps are now connected as shown in circuit 2. The 12·0 volt battery supplies a current of 0·40 ampere to this circuit.

12·0 volts

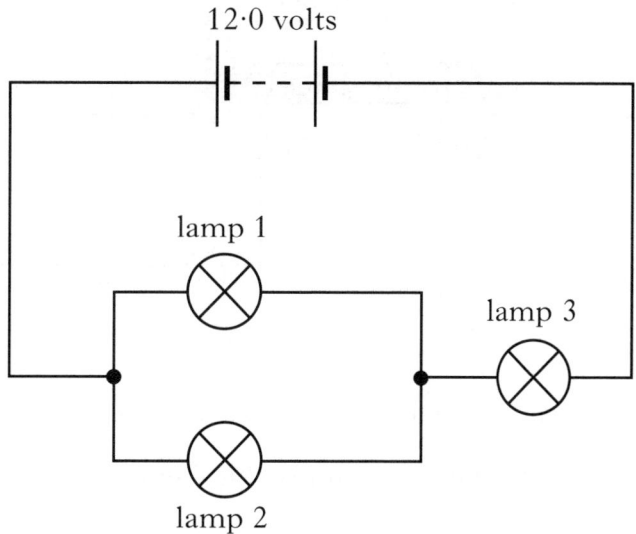

Circuit 2

(i) Complete the table to show the current in each lamp and the voltage across each lamp.

	Lamp 1	*Lamp 2*	*Lamp 3*
Voltage (volts)			8·0
Current (amperes)			0·4

2

(ii) Calculate the power dissipated in lamp 3.

Space for working and answer

2

(iii) State the **useful** energy change in this lamp.

....   **1**

Marks   K&U   P

9. The electrical energy used by a 48 watt heater is measured with a joulemeter as shown. The time taken to supply this energy is measured with a timer.

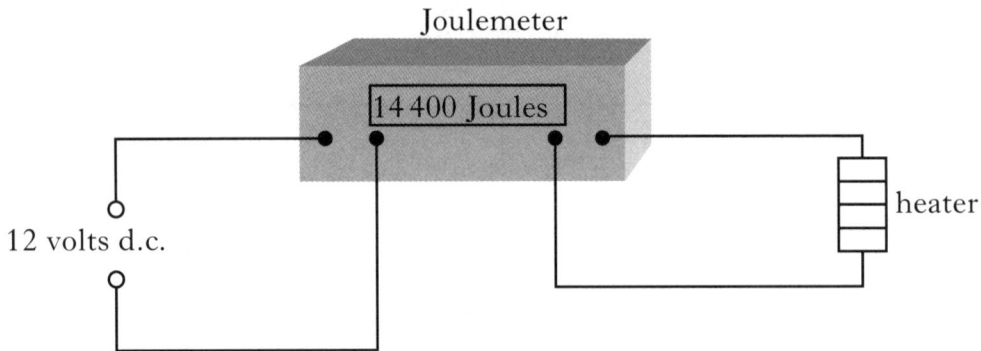

(a) The energy supplied is displayed on the joulemeter.

   (i) Calculate the time taken to supply this energy.

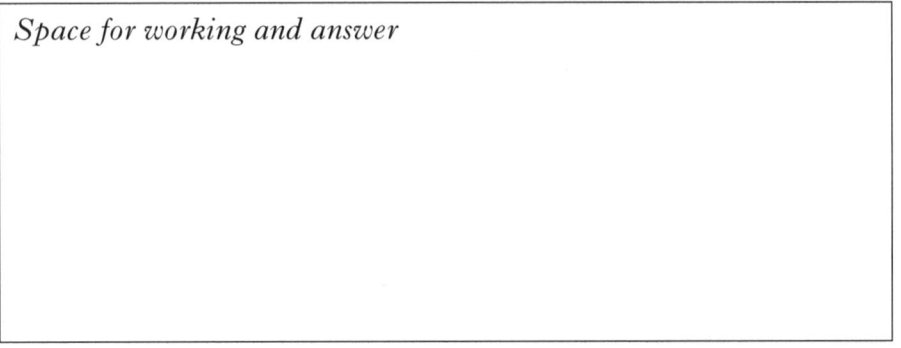

Space for working and answer

2

   (ii) The power supply provides direct current.

     Explain what is meant by direct current.

.... 1

OFFICIAL SQA PAST PAPERS 75 GENERAL PHYSICS 2010

Marks | K&U | PS

DO NOT
WRITE IN
THIS
MARGIN

9. (continued)

(b) Some household appliances are shown in the table.

(i) Complete the table using the correct power ratings from the list below.

60 watts   2800 watts   8000 watts

Appliance	*Power* (watts)
Kettle	
Bedside lamp	
Cooker	

1

(ii) Some appliances have an earth wire.

State the purpose of the earth wire.

....

....   1

[Turn over

Marks   K&U   P

10. A student uses a sound level meter to measure some sound levels.

The student records the results in the table.

Source of sound	Sound level (decibels)
school bell at 1 metre	100
inside a classroom	60
normal conversation	50
whisper	20

(a) (i) Humans can only hear sounds above a certain sound level.

What is the value of this sound level in decibels?

....   1

(ii) When one source of sound is twice as loud as another, the sound level increases by 10 decibels.

Which one of the **above sources** is twice as loud as the level of a normal conversation?

....   1

(b) The student measures the sound levels from earphones connected to an MP3 player.

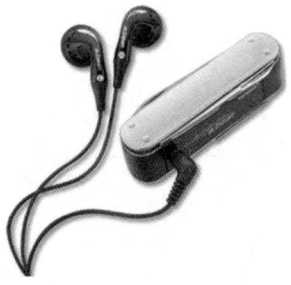

Sound levels up to 102 decibels are measured.

Explain why the student should reduce the sound level to below 80 decibels before wearing the earphones.

....   1

DO NOT
WRITE IN
THIS
MARGIN

Marks   K&U   PS

10.   **(continued)**

(c)   The student now measures the range of sound frequencies that humans can hear.

(i)   What name is given to high frequency sounds beyond the range of human hearing?

....   **1**

(ii)   Give **one** example of a use of these high frequency sounds in medicine.

....   **1**

[Turn over

Marks | K&U | P

11. Read the following passage.

In a hospital, a new digital X-ray imaging system is being used to replace photographic film. In the digital system, X-rays are detected by sensors and an image displayed on a computer screen.

Photographic film, which contains silver, is expensive and hazardous chemicals are used to develop the film. The digital system is less expensive, does not use hazardous chemicals and the X-ray image is obtained in a shorter time.

(*a*) Using information **given in the passage** state **two** advantages of the digital X-ray imaging system.

Advantage 1 ....

Advantage 2 .... **2**

(*b*)   (i) Hospital staff who operate X-ray machines wear film badges.

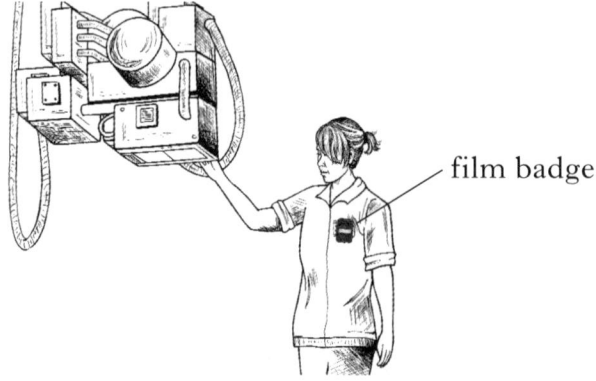

film badge

A film badge contains photographic film sealed in a plastic holder. Light cannot enter the film badge.

What effect does X-ray radiation have on photographic film?

.... **1**

(ii) Suggest a reason why hospital staff wear film badges.

.... **1**

Marks | K&U | PS

11. (continued)

(c) Another imaging system makes use of the invisible heat rays given out by the human body. The images produced by this system are called thermograms.

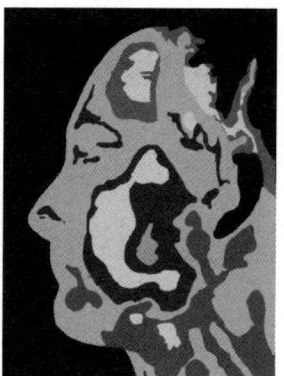

State the radiation used to make thermograms.

.... 1

[Turn over

Marks K&U P

12. (*a*) The circuit below can be used to light an LED after a short time delay. The capacitor is charged using the 5·0 volt supply.

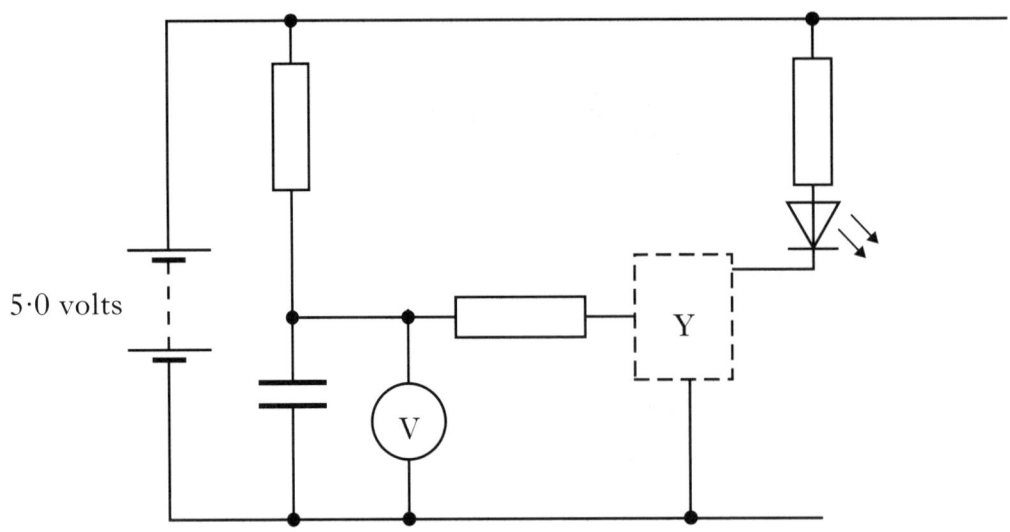

5·0 volts

(i) State what happens to the voltage across the capacitor when it charges.

.... **1**

(ii) Component Y is a transistor.

Draw the symbol for a transistor.

> *Space for drawing*

1

(iii) State the function of the transistor in this circuit.

.... **1**

Marks K&U PS

12. (continued)

(b) The circuit below is used to monitor temperature changes in a liquid. The thermistor is immersed in the liquid.

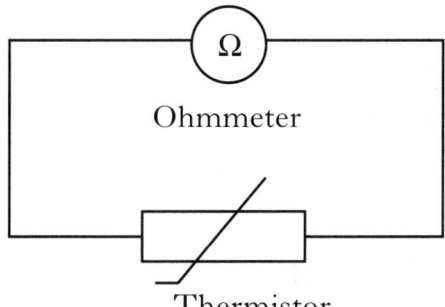

Ohmmeter

Thermistor

(i) State what happens to the reading on the ohmmeter as the liquid cools.

....   **1**

(ii) The thermistor is now connected to a battery and an ammeter as shown.

5·0 volts

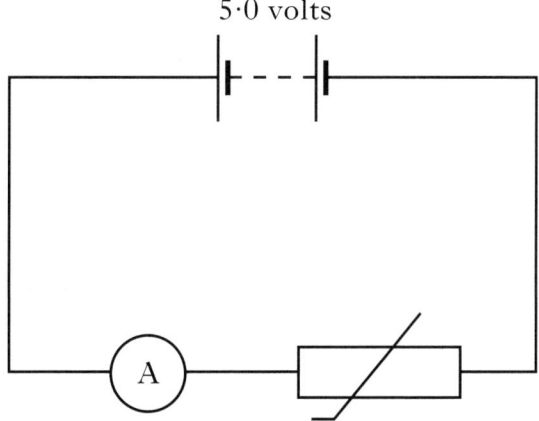

A

Calculate the current in the circuit when the resistance of the thermistor is 1000 ohms.

> *Space for working and answer*

2

[Turn over

Marks

K&U   P

13. Two identical LEDs are connected as shown in the circuit below.

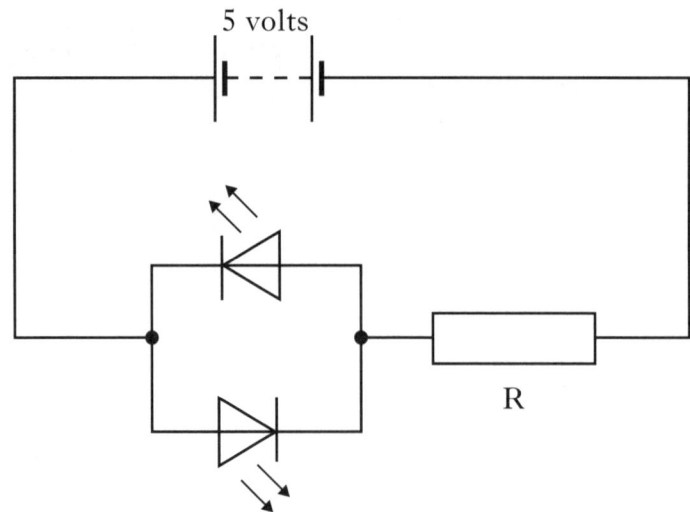

One LED fails to light. The circuit is complete and none of the components are faulty.

(a) (i) Explain why one LED does not light.

....   **1**

(ii) Explain why the series resistor R is needed.

....

....   **1**

(b) The table shows energy conversions that can take place in electronic output devices.

(i) Complete the table.

Energy in	Output device	Energy out
electrical		sound
electrical	LED	light
electrical		kinetic
electrical	heater	heat

1

(ii) Output devices can be analogue or digital.

Name **one** digital output device.

....   **1**

Marks K&U PS

14. A carriage on a roller coaster is pulled up the first slope.

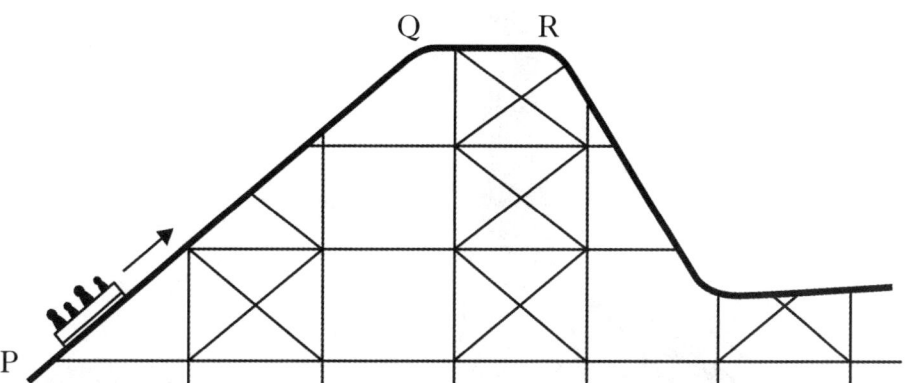

(*a*) The carriage is pulled up the slope from P to Q at a constant speed.

What can be said about the forces acting on the carriage as it is pulled up the slope?

.... **1**

(*b*) The carriage is released from rest at R. After a time of 2·5 seconds, the carriage has reached a speed of 14 metres per second.

Calculate the acceleration of the carriage.

Space for working and answer

2

(*c*) The carriage travels a total distance of 720 metres in a time of 100 seconds.

Calculate the average speed of the carriage.

Space for working and answer

2

Marks | K&U | P

15. A passenger at an airport pulls a suitcase towards the check-in desk.

(*a*) The suitcase has been designed to reduce the effects of friction when it is pulled.

(i) Explain how the suitcase has been designed to reduce friction.

.... **1**

(ii) Why is it important to reduce the force of friction on the suitcase?

.... **1**

(*b*) The suitcase is pulled for a distance of 15 metres using a force of 20 newtons.

Calculate the work done in pulling the suitcase.

Space for working and answer

2

Marks   K&U   PS

15.   **(continued)**

(c)   (i)   At the check-in desk, the suitcase is lifted through a vertical height of 0·4 metres onto a scale. The reading on the scale is 16 kilograms.

Calculate the gravitational potential energy gained by the suitcase when it is lifted onto the scale.

> *Space for working and answer*

2

(ii)   The maximum weight allowed for a suitcase is 150 newtons.

Is the weight of the suitcase within the weight limit?

You **must justify** your answer with a calculation.

> *Space for working and answer*

2

[Turn over

Marks K&U P

16. A thermal power station has an efficiency of 40%. A combined heat and power station is more efficient; it uses heat to produce hot water for homes as well as generating electrical energy. The energy output for each power station is shown in the diagrams below.

waste heat energy

40% electrical energy output

Thermal power station

20% waste heat energy

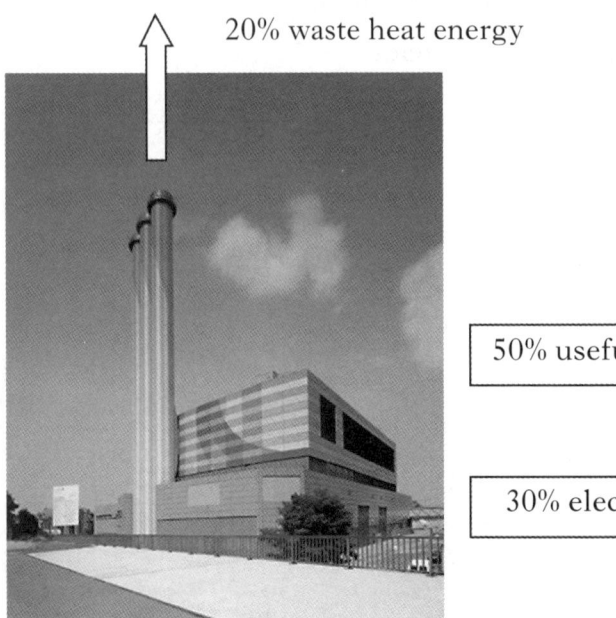

50% useful heat energy output

30% electrical energy output

Combined heat and power station

(*a*) (i) Calculate the percentage of waste heat for the **thermal power station**.

> *Space for working and answer*

1

Marks

16. (*a*) (continued)

(ii) Calculate the total percentage useful energy output of the **combined heat and power station**.

> *Space for working and answer*

1

(*b*) A combined heat and power station saves energy in the power industry.

(i) Describe **one** method of saving energy in the home.

.... 1

(ii) Describe **one** method of saving energy in transport.

.... 1

[Turn over

Marks | K&U | P:

17. Electrical power is distributed by the National Grid system. Transformers are used in this grid system.

(a) State why transformers are used in the grid.

.... 1

(b) The voltages required at various stages of the grid system are shown.

Stage	Voltage (volts)
Super Grid	400 000
National Grid	132 000
Heavy industry	33 000
Light industry	11 000
Homes	230

A transformer transfers power from the National Grid to heavy industry. The primary coil of the transformer has 6000 turns.

(i) State the voltage input at the primary coil.

.... 1

(ii) State the voltage output at the secondary coil.

.... 1

(iii) Calculate the number of turns in the secondary coil.

Space for working and answer

2

Marks K&U PS

18. An astronomer uses a refracting telescope to study the Moon.

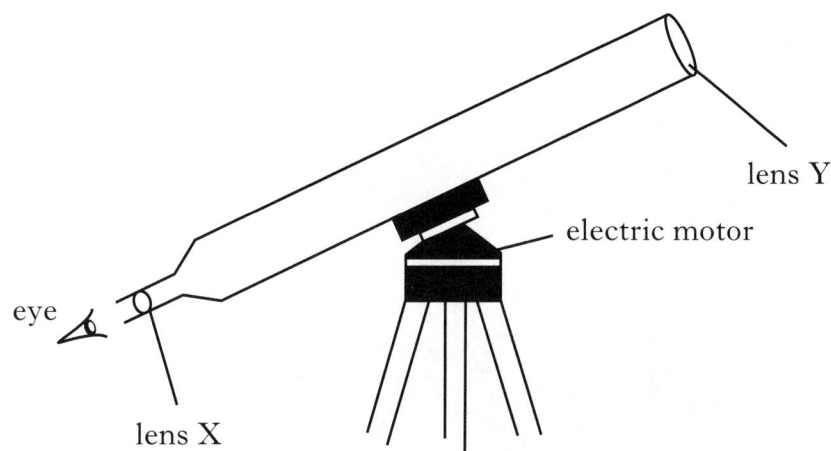

(a) The telescope has two convex lenses.

Name each of the lenses.

lens X ....

lens Y **2**

(b) An electric motor turns the telescope to keep it pointing at the Moon.

Suggest a reason why the telescope must turn to keep it pointing at the Moon.

....

....   **1**

(c) Put the following in order of increasing size.

galaxy   solar system   planet   universe

smallest   ....

                 ....

                 ....

largest **2**

[Turn over

Marks   K&U   P

19. A water rocket consists of a plastic bottle containing air and water.

A bicycle pump is used to increase the pressure of the air in the bottle. When the pressure is high enough the plastic bottle is fired upwards.

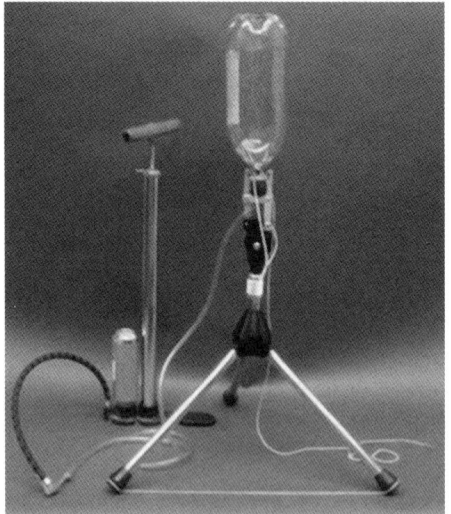

(a) (i) The air inside the plastic bottle exerts a downward force on the water.

Describe the force exerted by the water.

....   **1**

(ii) At one stage of the flight, the rocket has a mass of 0·70 kilograms. The unbalanced force on the rocket is 2·1 newtons.

Calculate the acceleration of the rocket.

Space for working and answer

2

(b) A space rocket can escape the gravitational pull of the Earth if the rocket engine has enough thrust.

An identical rocket would need less thrust if it is launched from the Moon.

Explain why less thrust is needed if the rocket is launched from the Moon.

....   **1**

DO NOT
WRITE IN
THIS
MARGIN

Marks | K&U | PS

19. (continued)

(c) Some spacecraft go into orbit around the Earth after they are launched.

(i) Name the force that acts downwards on a spacecraft in orbit.

.... **1**

(ii) Name the force that causes the spacecraft to heat up when it re-enters the Earth's atmosphere.

.... **1**

[END OF QUESTION PAPER]

ADDITIONAL SPACE FOR ANSWERS

Make sure you write the correct question number beside each answer.

ADDITIONAL SPACE FOR ANSWERS

Make sure you write the correct question number beside each answer.

K&U	PS

DO NOT
WRITE I
THIS
MARGI

K&U P

ADDITIONAL SPACE FOR ANSWERS

Make sure you write the correct question number beside each answer.

K&U P

STANDARD GRADE | GENERAL

2011

[BLANK PAGE]

FOR OFFICIAL USE

K&U   PS

G

3220/401

NATIONAL
QUALIFICATIONS
2011

MONDAY, 23 MAY
9.00 AM – 10.30 AM

PHYSICS
STANDARD GRADE
General Level

Fill in these boxes and read what is printed below.

Full name of centre

Town

Forename(s)

Surname

Date of birth

Day	Month	Year

Scottish candidate number

Number of seat

Reference may be made to the Physics Data Booklet.

1   All questions should be answered.

2   The questions may be answered in any order but all answers must be written clearly and legibly in this book.

3   For questions 1–5, write down, in the space provided, the letter corresponding to the answer you think is correct. There is only **one** correct answer.

4   For questions 6–19, write your answer where indicated by the question or in the space provided after the question.

5   If you change your mind about your answer you may score it out and replace it in the space provided at the end of the answer book.

6   If you use the additional space at the end of the answer book for answering any questions, you **must** write the correct question number beside each answer.

7   Before leaving the examination room you must give this book to the Invigilator. If you do not, you may lose all the marks for this paper.

Use **blue** or **black ink**. Pencil may be used for graphs and diagrams only.

SA 3220/401 6/19210

1. The purpose of the curved reflector on a satellite television aerial is to

   A   make the transmitted signal stronger

   B   make the received signal stronger

   C   reflect light onto the receiver

   D   absorb transmitted signals

   E   absorb received signals.

Answer ☐   **1**

2. Which diagram shows the correct paths for the rays forming an inverted image?

A

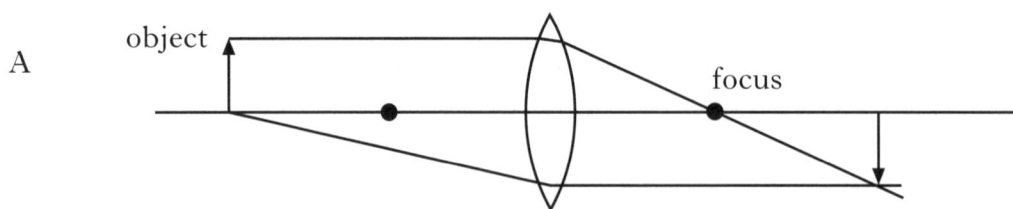

B

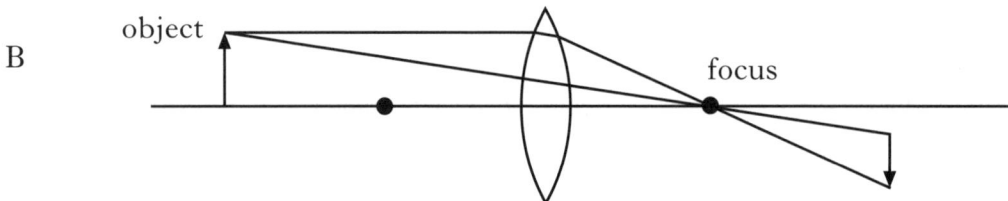

C

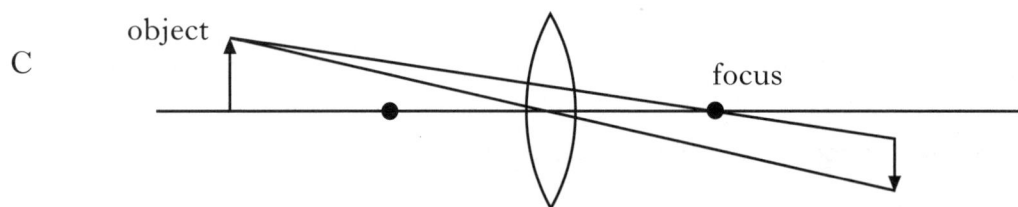

D

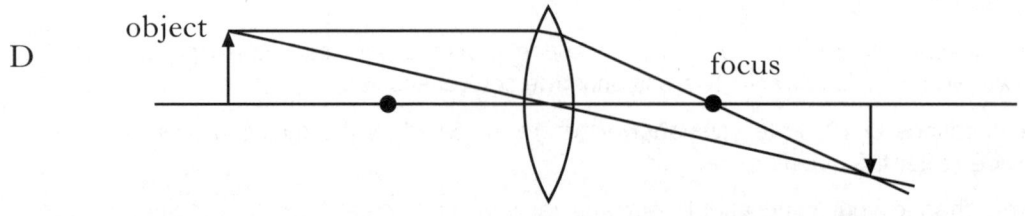

E

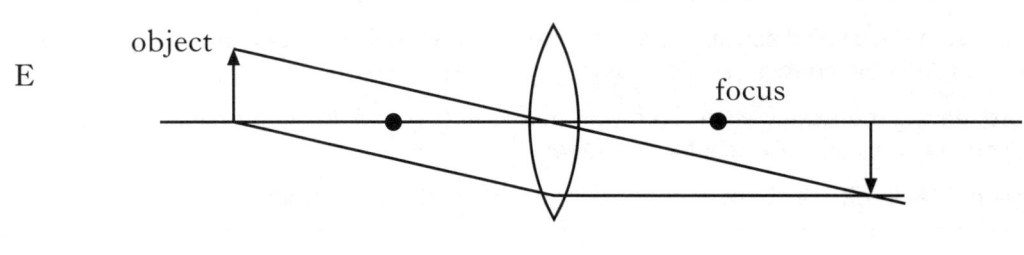

Answer ☐   **1**

3. Which of the following is the correct symbol for a light emitting diode (LED)?

A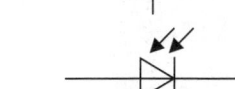

B

C

D

E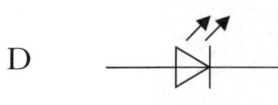

Answer ☐   1

4. A substance is changing state from a liquid to a solid.

Which row in the table gives the correct description of the effect on the temperature and the heat energy of the substance?

	Temperature	Heat Energy
A	stays the same	no effect
B	stays the same	given out by substance
C	increases	taken in by substance
D	decreases	given out by substance
E	decreases	taken in by substance

Answer ☐   1

5. Far out in space the rocket motor of a space probe is fired for a short time.

When the motor is switched off, the probe will

A   decelerate until it stops

B   follow a curved path

C   continue to accelerate forwards

D   move at a constant speed

E   change direction.

Answer ☐   1

Marks | K&U | P

6. The River Severn in England is a tidal river. At certain times the tide does not rise gradually, but instead tidal waves travel along the river. Surfing these waves is a popular activity.

(*a*) One tidal wave travels 34 km along the river in a time of two and a half hours.

Calculate the average speed of the tidal wave in km/h.

> *Space for working and answer*

2

DO NOT WRITE IN THIS MARGIN

Marks K&U PS

6. (continued)

(b) A surfer is gathering data about these tidal waves.

(i) The surfer stands beside the river and counts 8 waves passing a point in a time of 10 seconds.

Calculate the frequency of these waves.

Space for working and answer

2

(ii) As the waves move from the sea to the river, their wavelength decreases and their amplitude increases.

The drawing shows waves in the sea.

Sketch the waves as they would appear in the river.

You must show clearly differences in wavelength and amplitude in your sketch.

Space for drawing

2

[Turn over

7. Messages can be sent using codes.

(*a*) Two friends, living in neighbouring houses, set up a communication system using wires. They can send and receive simple coded messages using this system.

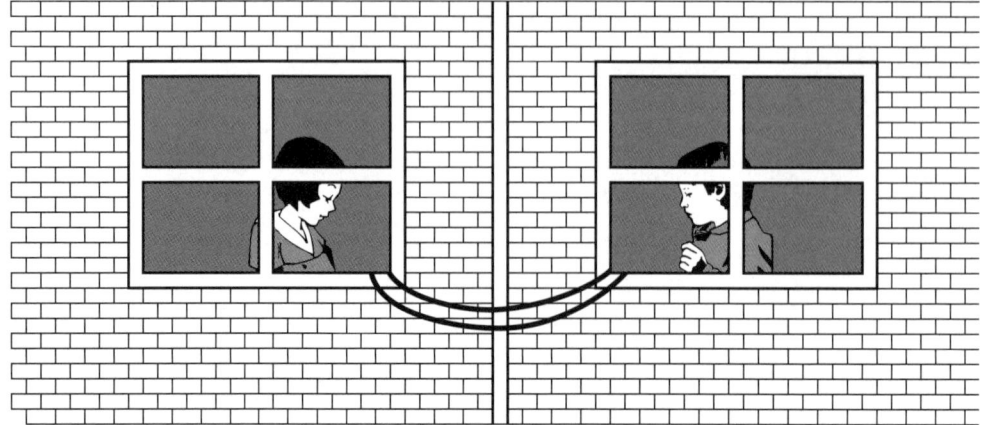

The diagram shows one of the electrical circuits that the friends use.

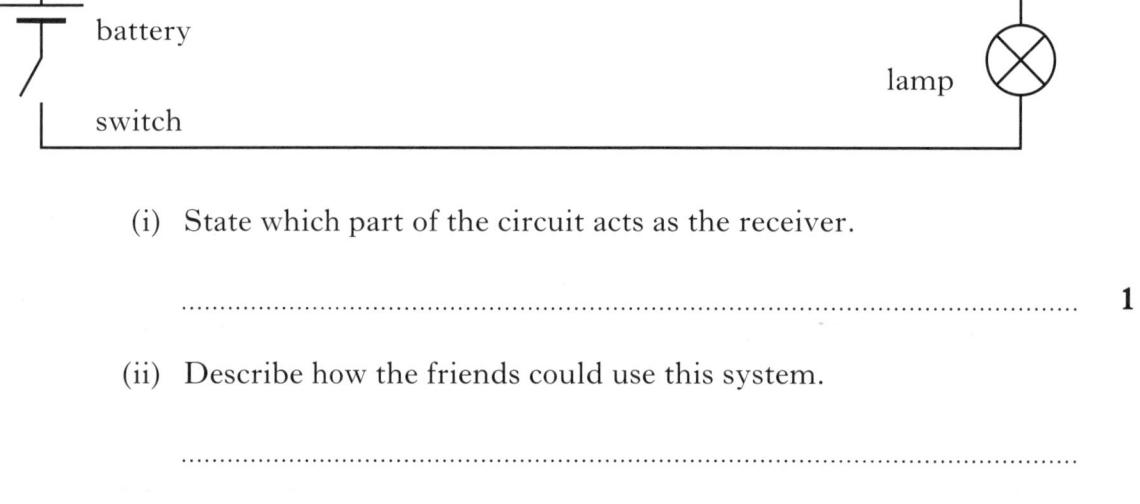

(i) State which part of the circuit acts as the receiver.

.... **1**

(ii) Describe how the friends could use this system.

....

.... **2**

Marks

7. (continued)

(b) The pilot of a light aircraft can use a code to navigate between ground stations.

Each station transmits a different coded radio signal which the pilot can hear.

(i) The block diagram shows the main parts of a radio receiver.

The labels in two of the blocks are missing.

Complete the block diagram by filling in the two missing labels.

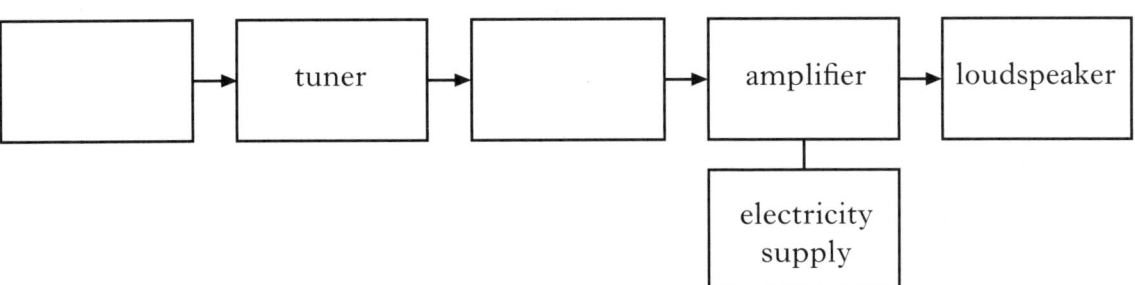

(ii) State the function of:

(A) the electricity supply;

.... 1

(B) the tuner.

.... 1

[Turn over

Marks K&U P

8. A student sets up an experiment to investigate the current in and the voltage across two different resistors.

The student uses a battery, an ammeter, a voltmeter and some wires to obtain measurements for each resistor.

(*a*) Complete the diagram shown below, by inserting a resistor, to show how the measurements could be obtained.

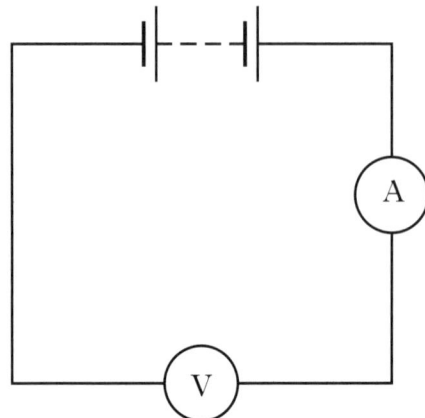

1

(*b*) The measurements obtained for each resistor are shown in the table.

Resistor	Current (amperes)	Voltage (volts)
X	0·6	1·5
Y	7·5	1·5

(i) Use the information in the table to calculate the resistance of resistor Y.

Space for working and answer

2

Marks   K&U   PS

8. **(*b*) (continued)**

(ii) Complete the sentence below by circling the correct phrase.

An increase in the resistance of a circuit leads to $\left\{\begin{array}{l}\text{an increase}\\\text{no change}\\\text{a decrease}\end{array}\right\}$

in the current in that circuit.   **1**

[Turn over

Marks K&U P

9. The diagram shows a hair straightener and its rating plate.

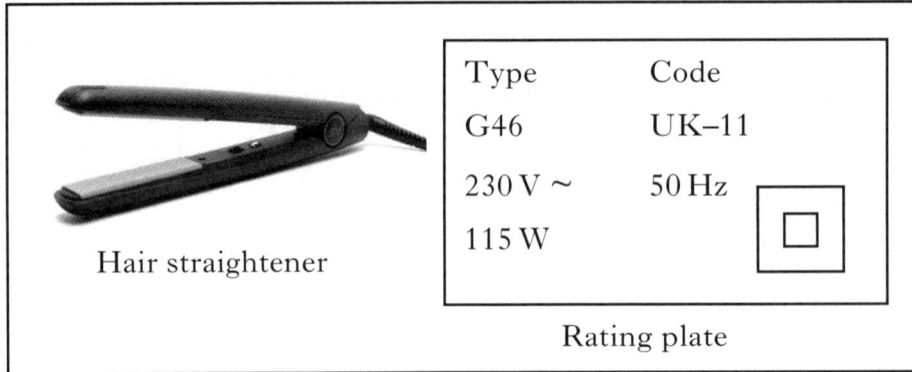

Type	Code
G46	UK–11
230 V ~	50 Hz
115 W	

Hair straightener

Rating plate

(a) (i) State the names of the wires in the flex of the hair straightener.

.... **1**

(ii) State the colours of the insulation on the wires in this flex.
You must indicate clearly which colour applies to each wire.

.... **1**

(b) Calculate the current in the hair straightener when it is operating at its stated power rating.

Space for working and answer

2

(c) (i) State the correct fuse value which should be in the plug of the hair straightener.

.... **1**

(ii) State the purpose of the fuse in the plug.

.... **1**

Marks

K&U | PS

10. A student investigates the properties of two thermometers. This student places the sterilised thermometers under the armpits of a second student for two minutes. Temperature readings are recorded at 15 second intervals for four minutes.

The graphs show the recorded readings.

Thermometer A

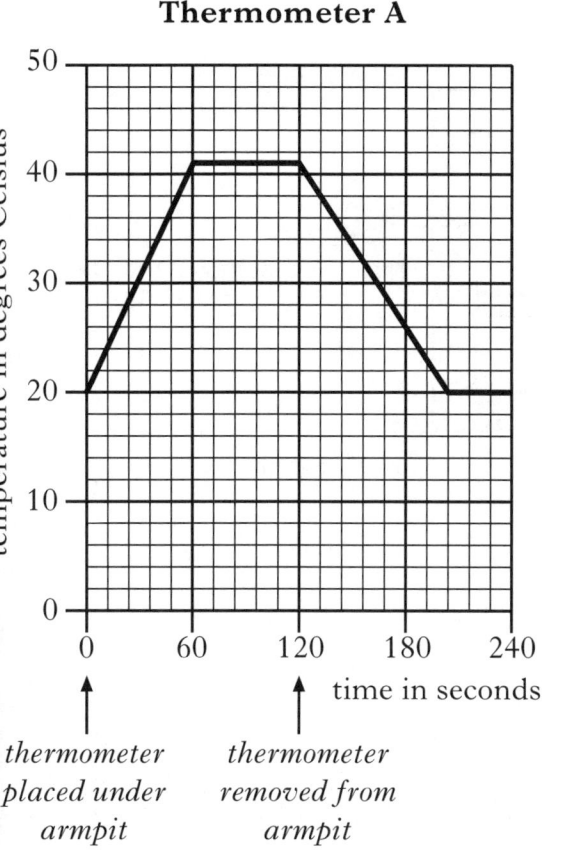

Thermometer B

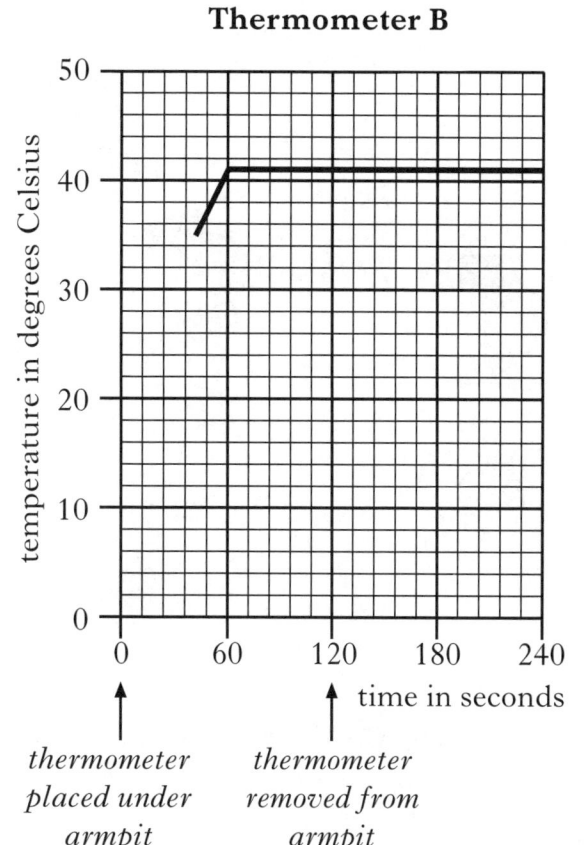

(a) Both thermometers are made of glass and contain a column of liquid.

Explain how a liquid in glass thermometer works.

....

....   **1**

(b) (i) State which thermometer is a clinical thermometer.

....   **1**

(ii) Referring to the graphs, give **two** reasons for your choice.

....

....   **2**

(c) Explain why these results suggest that the student may be ill.

....

....   **1**

DO NOT
WRITE I
THIS
MARGIN

Marks K&U P

11. In a class experiment, some students investigate their range of hearing.

A signal generator is connected to a loudspeaker and the teacher checks that all students can hear the sound. The frequency of the sound signal is then gradually increased.

The volume is kept constant.

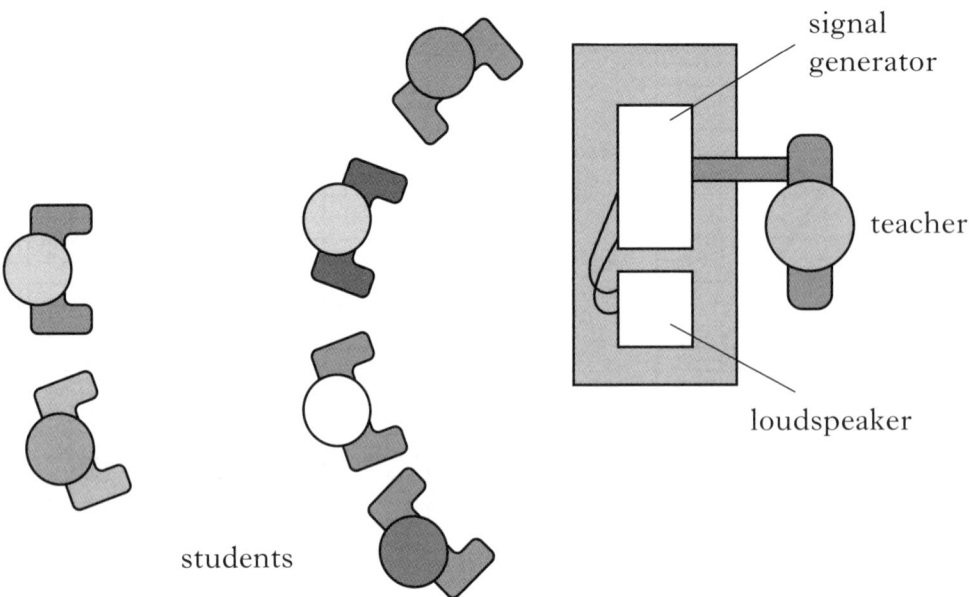

signal
generator

teacher

loudspeaker

students

(*a*) (i) State why this test is not a fair one.

.... **1**

(ii) The frequency of the sound signal reaches 20 000 Hz.

No students can hear this signal.

What name is given to high frequency vibrations that are above the range of human hearing?

.... **1**

(*b*) One student repeats the experiment using a stethoscope. The earpieces of the stethoscope are in the student's ears. The student places the open bell of the stethoscope on the table next to the loudspeaker.

Explain how the stethoscope makes the sound heard by the student louder.

....

....

....

.... **2**

Marks

12. Two logic systems, A and B, for controlling door opening mechanisms are shown.

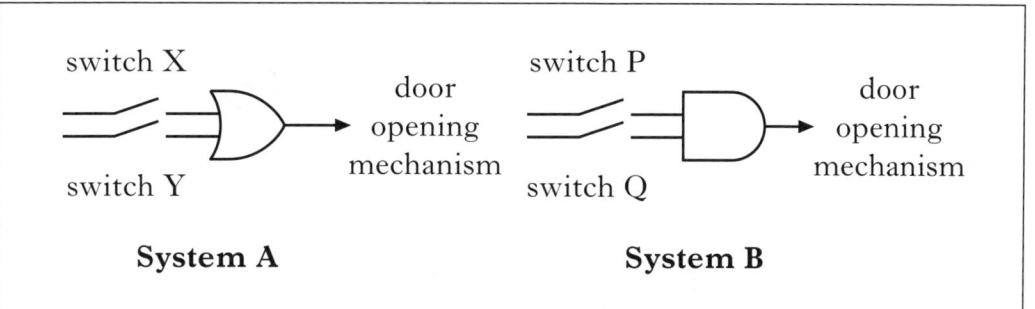

System A   **System B**

To open the passenger doors on a train, the button marked "Open Doors When Illuminated" must be pressed. To illuminate the button the conductor closes a master switch using a key.

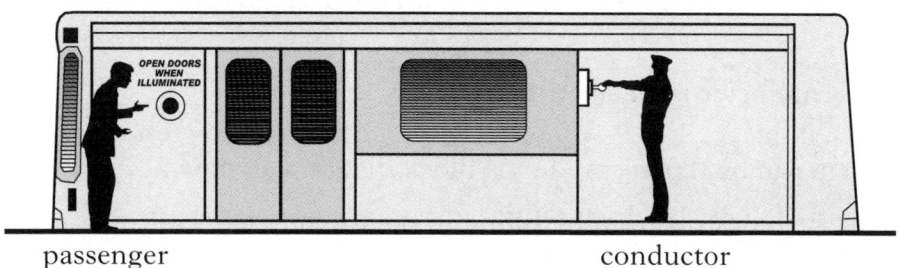

passenger   conductor

(a) Explain which system, A or B, should be used in this situation.

....

....   **2**

(b) The main entrance doors in a school can be opened by either of two office staff using a switch on their desk.

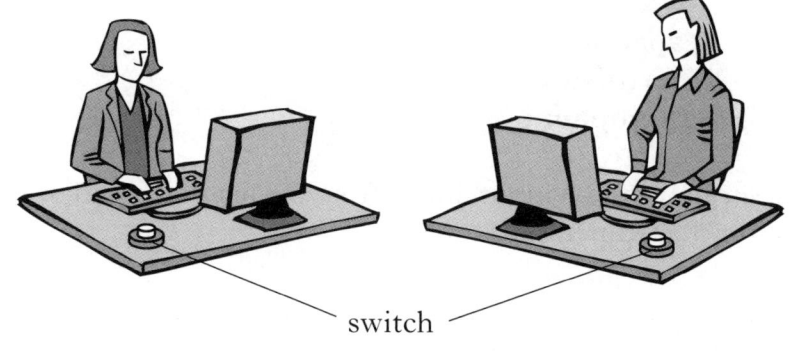

switch

Explain which system, A or B, should be used in this situation.

....

....   **2**

Marks

13. A supermarket uses an open display cabinet which keeps fresh food cold.

The temperature of the cabinet is monitored and displayed using a digital thermometer.

The digital thermometer is an electronic system.

(*a*) This system can be represented by a block diagram as shown.

Complete the block diagram by filling in the missing label.

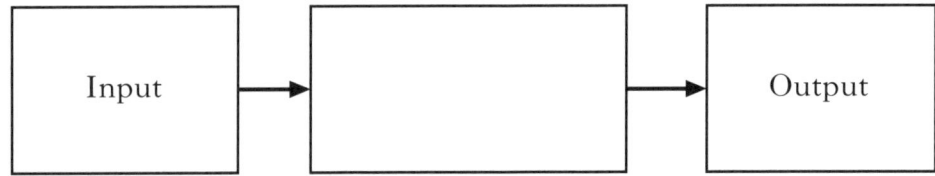

1

(*b*) The list below shows the names of some input devices.

light dependent resistor (LDR)
switch
capacitor
thermistor
microphone

(i) Choose an appropriate input device from the list that could be used to monitor the temperature.

.... 1

(ii) Suggest an output device that could be used to display the temperature.

.... 1

Marks K&U PS

13. (continued)

(c) A public address system is used in the supermarket to make announcements.

The public address system uses an amplifier. An engineer is testing the amplifier by applying different input voltages.

The output voltages are measured and the data is shown on the graph.

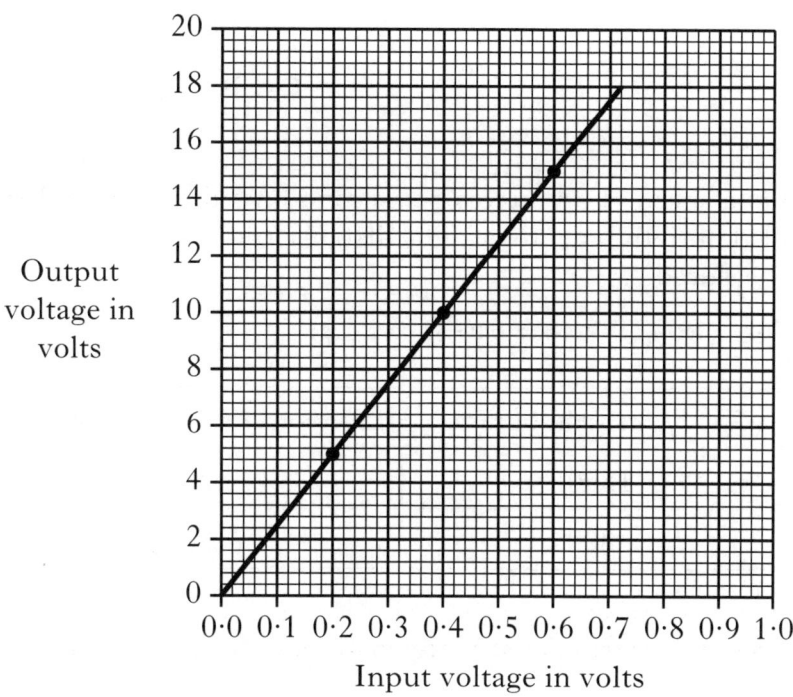

Using values from the graph, calculate the voltage gain of the amplifier.

Space for working and answer

2

(d) The test signal applied to the input of the amplifier has a frequency of 1000 Hz.

State the frequency of the test signal at the output of the amplifier.

....   1

DO NOT
WRITE I
THIS
MARGIN

Marks   K&U   P

14. A motoring journalist tests the grip on two new designs of tyre.

One set of tyres is placed on car A, the other set of tyres is placed on car B.

Car A   **Car B**

Each car is driven at a speed of 28 metres per second on a dry surface then the brakes are applied until the car stops. The distance travelled by each car during braking is measured.

The table gives information about the cars.

Car	Mass of car in kilograms	Braking distance in metres
A	1500	70
B	800	50

(a) Car B decelerates at 8 metres per second per second during braking.

   (i) Calculate the force required during braking.

   Space for working and answer

2

   (ii) Calculate the work done on Car B during braking.

   Space for working and answer

2

DO NOT WRITE IN THIS MARGIN

Marks K&U PS

14. (continued)

(*b*) The journalist concludes that the tyres on Car B have better grip than those on Car A.

Explain why the journalist's conclusion may not be correct.

.... **1**

[Turn over

Marks | K&U | P

15. A scientist studies a flea while it jumps.

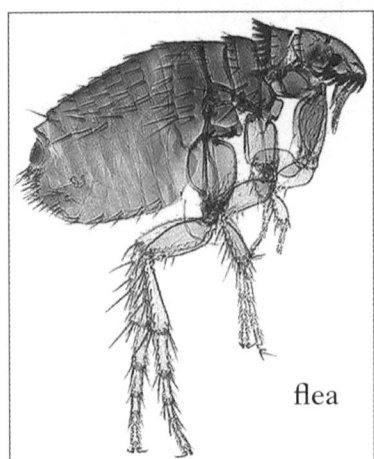

flea

Starting from rest, the flea accelerates to 1·2 metres per second in a time of 0·001 seconds.

The flea has a mass of 0·0001 kilograms.

(a) State the meaning of the term "acceleration".

.... **1**

(b) Calculate the acceleration of the flea.

Space for working and answer

2

(c) Calculate the weight of the flea.

Space for working and answer

2

[Turn over for Question 16 on *Page twenty*

Marks | K&U | P

16. A hydroelectric power station uses water stored in a dam to generate electricity.

The power station generates electricity at 16 000 volts. Electricity is then transmitted across the country at 275 000 volts using the National Grid.

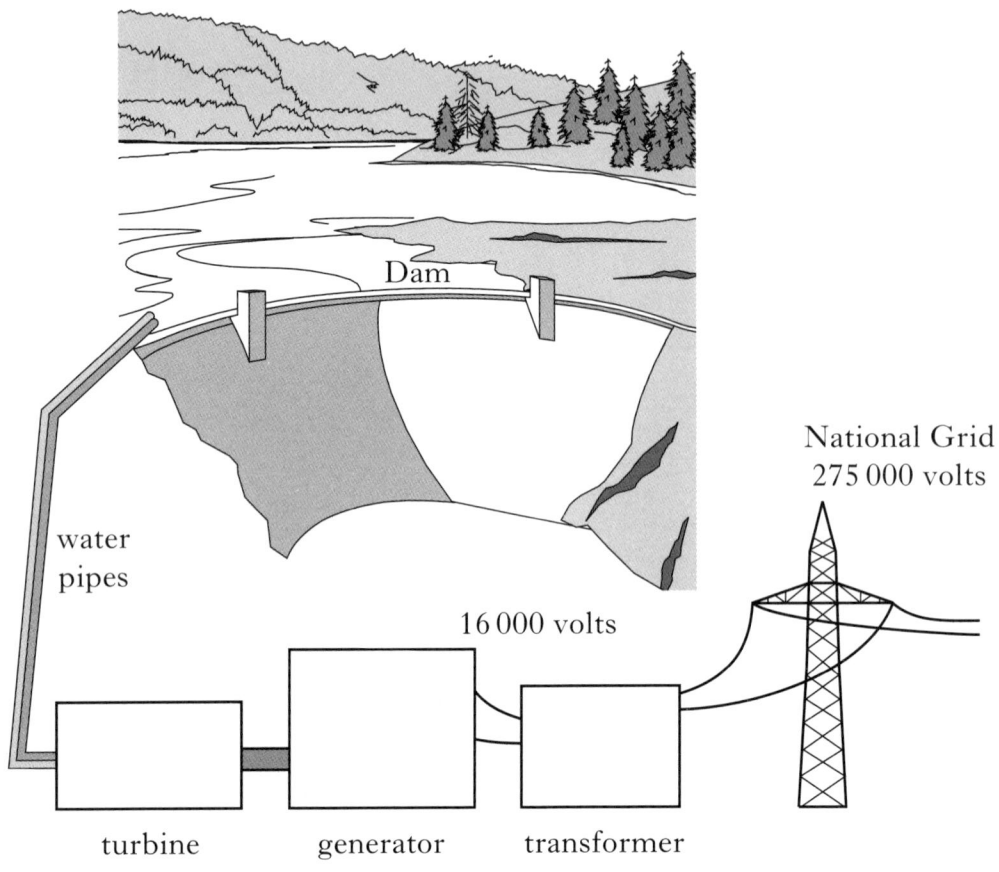

(*a*) State the energy transformation:

   (i) in the water pipes;

   .... **1**

   (ii) at the generator.

   .... **1**

Marks

16. (continued)

(b) (i) A transformer consists of three parts.

Label each of these three parts on the diagram, using the names below.

core   **secondary coil**   **primary coil**

electricity from generator

electricity to National Grid

2

(ii) The transformer has 18 000 turns on the primary coil.

Calculate the number of turns on the secondary coil.

Space for working and answer

2

(iii) Why is electrical power transmitted at a very high voltage across the National Grid?

....

1

[Turn over

Marks K&U   P

17. A scientific research station near the South Pole uses a vertical axis windmill to generate electrical power.

(*a*) During a 24 hour period the average power output of the wind-powered generator is 25 kilowatts.

Calculate the electrical energy generated in kilowatt-hours during this time.

Space for working and answer

2

Marks | K&U | PS

17. (continued)

(b) The research station uses 200 kilowatt-hours of energy in a 24 hour period.

The remaining energy is sold at 9 pence per kilowatt-hour to another station.

Calculate the income from the sale of this remaining energy.

Space for working and answer

3

(c) Wind is a renewable source of energy.

Name **one** other renewable source of energy.

.... **1**

[Turn over

Marks K&U P$

18. A spacecraft is orbiting the Earth. Scientists prepare to bring it back to the Earth's surface.

(a) To safely enter the Earth's atmosphere, the speed of the spacecraft must be decreased. This is achieved by thruster rockets.

The spacecraft has a mass of 6000 kilograms and the thruster rockets create a combined thrust of 4800 newtons.

Calculate the deceleration of the spacecraft when the thruster rockets fire.

Space for working and answer

2

(b) A heat resistant tile breaks off the spacecraft. The force of gravity near the Earth causes both the spacecraft and the tile to accelerate towards the Earth.

(i) Complete the sentence by circling the correct phrase.

If there is no air resistance the tile will accelerate

at $\left\{ \begin{array}{l} \text{a lower rate than} \\ \text{the same rate as} \\ \text{a faster rate than} \end{array} \right\}$ the spacecraft.

1

(ii) When the objects enter the Earth's atmosphere some of their kinetic energy is transformed into heat.

Name the force that causes this energy transformation.

....

1

18. (continued)

(*c*) Not all of the spacecraft's kinetic energy is lost at re-entry. It still needs to be slowed down before impact with the Earth. This is achieved using a parachute.

The graph shows how the speed of a spacecraft changes from re-entry to impact.

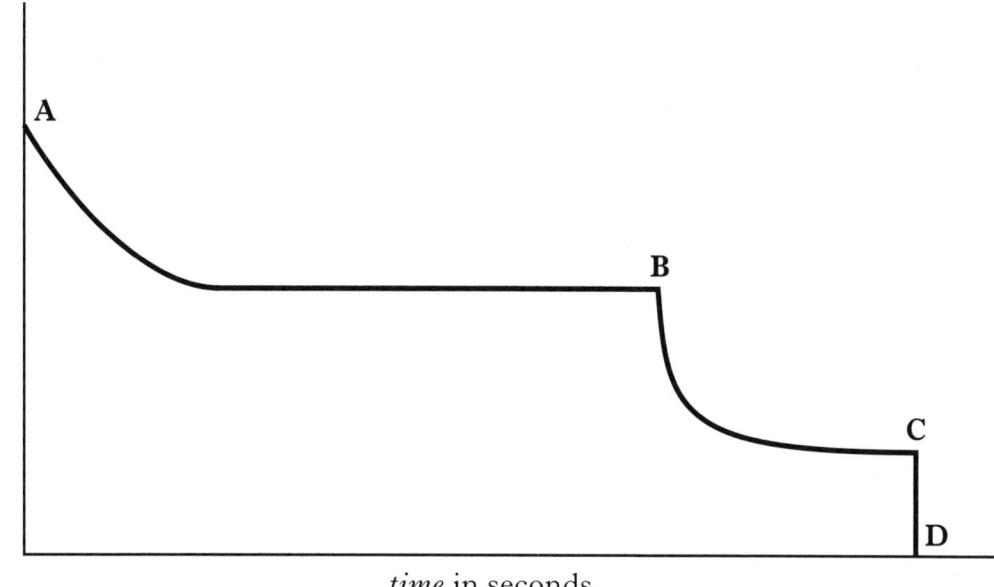

Which point on the graph corresponds to the parachute opening?

....   **1**

[Turn over for Question 19 on *Page twenty-six*

Marks

19. Read the following passage about comets.

Halley's Comet is famous because it is visible to the naked eye, orbiting from beyond the planet Neptune and returning to the solar system on average once every 76 years.

Halley's Comet last visited the inner solar system in 1986. It will return again in 2061.

Comets are made of ice mixed with frozen methane; substances very similar to those found on a moon called Miranda.

Comets can only survive very far away from the Sun. Most comets reside in the Oort Cloud which contains many billions of comets. The Oort Cloud reaches a quarter of the distance from the Sun to the next nearest star called Proxima Centauri.

The Oort Cloud is easily affected by the gravitational pull of the Milky Way galaxy which causes comets to move into new orbits that carry them closer to the Sun.

(a) Use information **given in the passage** to answer the following questions.

(i) State the name of **one** object that orbits a planet.

....   1

(ii) State the name of **one** object that generates light.

....   1

(iii) State the name of the object furthest away from the Earth.

....   1

(iv) State the name of **one** object that orbits the Sun.

....   1

(b) State what is meant by the term galaxy.

....   1

(c) State what is meant by the term solar system.

....   1

[END OF QUESTION PAPER]

DO NOT WRITE IN THIS MARGIN

K&U | PS

ADDITIONAL SPACE FOR ANSWERS

Make sure you write the correct question number beside each answer.

[BLANK PAGE]

STANDARD GRADE | GENERAL

2012

[BLANK PAGE]

FOR OFFICIAL USE

K&U   PS   **G**

NATIONAL QUALIFICATIONS 2012

PHYSICS
STANDARD GRADE
General Level

MONDAY, 30 APRIL
9.00 AM – 10.30 AM

3220/29/01

Fill in these boxes and read what is printed below.

Full name of centre

Town

Forename(s)

Surname

Number of seat

Date of birth
Day   Month   Year   Scottish candidate number

Reference may be made to the Physics Data Booklet.

1   All questions should be answered.

2   The questions may be answered in any order but all answers must be written clearly and legibly in this book.

3   For questions 1–5, write down, in the space provided, the letter corresponding to the answer you think is correct. There is only **one** correct answer.

4   For questions 6–19, write your answer where indicated by the question or in the space provided after the question.

5   If you change your mind about your answer you may score it out and replace it in the space provided at the end of the answer book.

6   If you use the additional space at the end of the answer book for answering any questions, you **must** write the correct question number beside each answer.

7   Before leaving the examination room you must give this book to the Invigilator. If you do not, you may lose all the marks for this paper.

Use **blue** or **black ink**. Pencil may be used for graphs and diagrams only.

1. In a radio, the tuner is used to

    A   select one signal from all the signals reaching the radio

    B   make the electrical signal stronger

    C   supply electrical energy to the radio

    D   change electrical energy to sound energy

    E   detect all the signals reaching the radio.

    Answer ☐   **1**

2. A student looks at the letter R on a piece of paper. The image formed on the student's retina is

    A

    B

    C

    D

    E

    Answer ☐   **1**

DO NOT WRITE IN THIS MARGIN

K&U | PS

3. Which of the following is the circuit symbol for an OR gate?

A

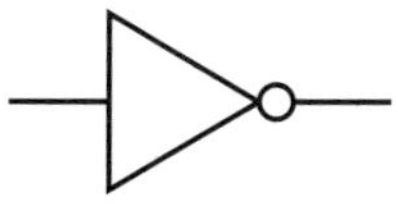

B

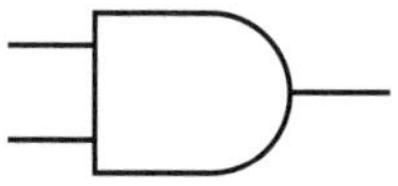

C

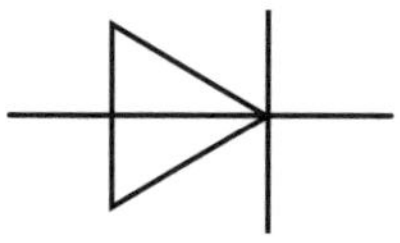

D

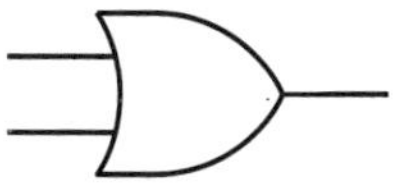

E

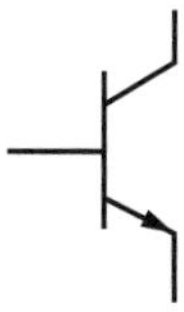

Answer ☐   1

4. Which term describes an object which orbits a star?

A   moon

B   planet

C   solar system

D   galaxy

E   universe

Answer ☐   1

5. A 5 kilogram mass is hung on a Newton balance and both are allowed to fall freely. What is the reading on the balance while the mass and balance are falling?

A   0 Newtons

B   5 Newtons

C   50 Newtons

D   500 Newtons

E   5000 Newtons

Answer ☐   1

6.   (*a*)   The telephone is one method of communicating by wires. A telephone handset contains an earpiece and a mouthpiece as shown.

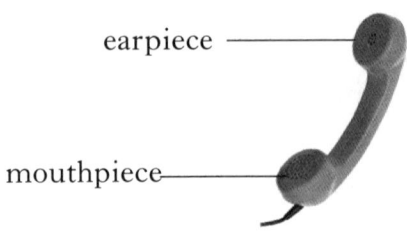

earpiece

mouthpiece

(i)   State the device used in the mouthpiece.

....   1

(ii)   State the energy change in this device.

....   1

(*b*)   The mouthpiece of a telephone is connected to an oscilloscope. A student whistles into the mouthpiece four times and the patterns produced on the oscilloscope are shown.

The oscilloscope settings are not altered between each whistle.

A 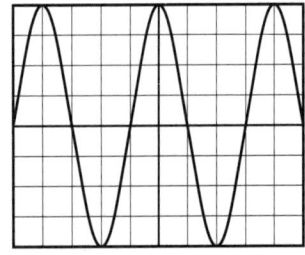   B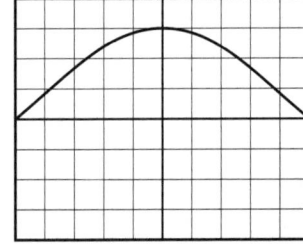

C 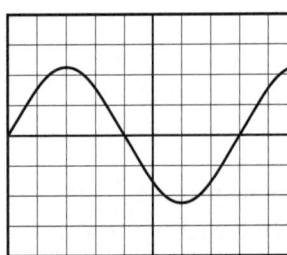   D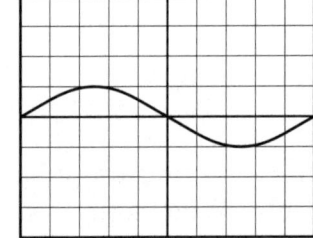

Which pattern is caused by:

(i)   the lowest frequency sound;

....   1

(ii)   the quietest sound?

....   1

7. A duck lands in a large pond and produces water waves. A 2·5 metre section of the pond is shown.

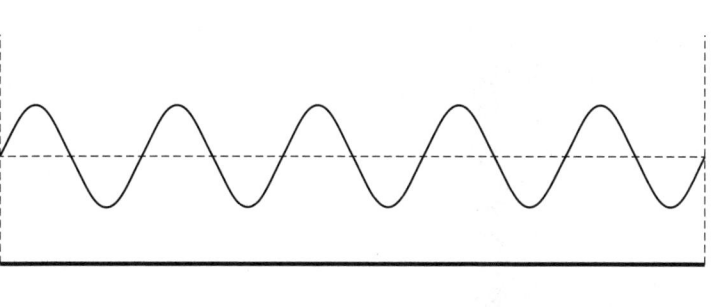

2·5 metres

(a) Calculate the wavelength of the waves.

Space for working and answer

2

(b) The frequency of the waves produced in the pond is 2 hertz.

Calculate the speed of these waves.

Space for working and answer

2

(c) Explain why the amplitude is smaller when the waves reach the other side of the pond.

1

8. A halogen heater contains four heater tubes which can be switched on separately or all together. The heater is mains operated.

(*a*) When one heating tube is switched on the current is 1·25 amperes and the voltage across the tube is 230 volts.

Calculate the resistance of the tube.

Space for working and answer

2

8. (continued)

(*b*) During cold weather the heater is used to heat a large conservatory.

conservatory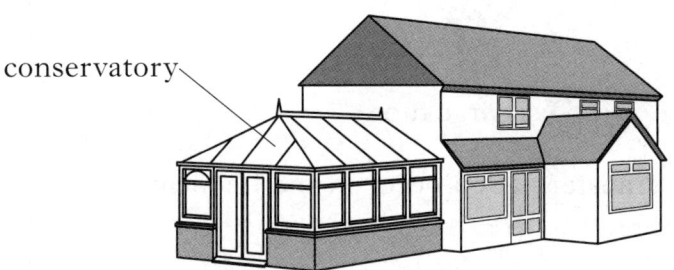

The heater is switched on at its highest setting.

At this setting the heater has a power rating of 1600 watts.

The heater is operated for 8 hours each day for one week.

Calculate the energy in kilowatt-hours used by the heater in this week.

> *Space for working and answer*

2

(*c*) A fault develops in the halogen heater circuit. A technician uses a continuity tester to test the fuse from the plug. The continuity tester contains a lamp and a battery.

Complete the circuit diagram to show the continuity tester connected to the fuse.

> *Space for diagram*
>
>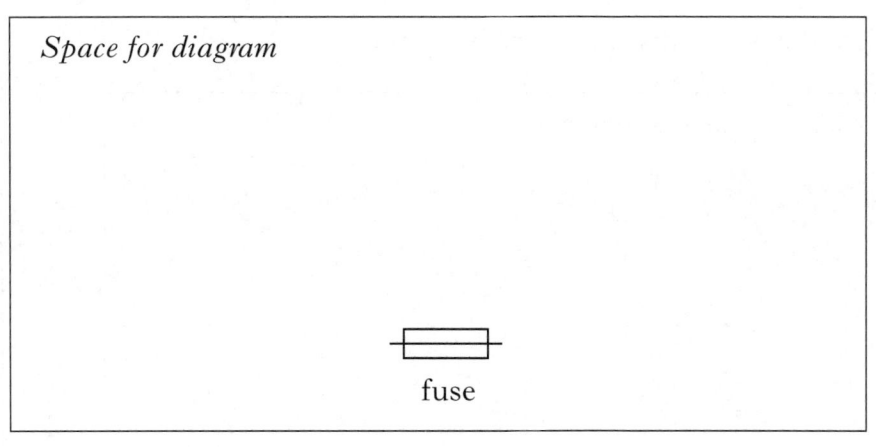
>
> fuse

2

9. A student compares two different sources of light.

Filament lamp

Discharge tube

(a) Where does the energy transformation occur in the filament lamp?

.... **1**

(b) Why is a discharge tube more efficient than a filament lamp?

.... **1**

(c) The student sets up the following experiment to investigate the power of a filament lamp.

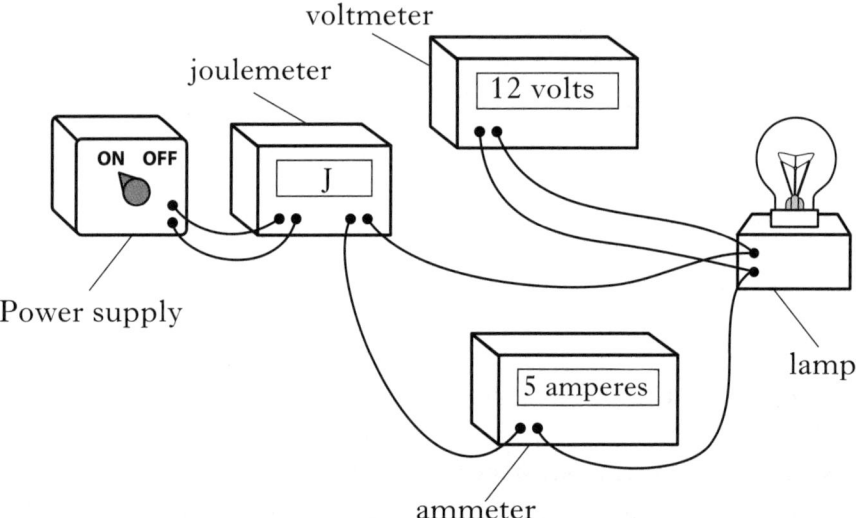

The reading on the voltmeter is 12 volts and the reading on the ammeter is 5 amperes.

Calculate the power dissipated in the lamp.

Space for working and answer

2

9. **(continued)**

(d) The student examines the following images.

Explain why each situation is dangerous.

(i)

.... **1**

(ii)

.... **1**

[Turn over

10. (*a*) A simple model of the atom is shown.

Label the diagram to show the **electrons** and **protons** in this model.

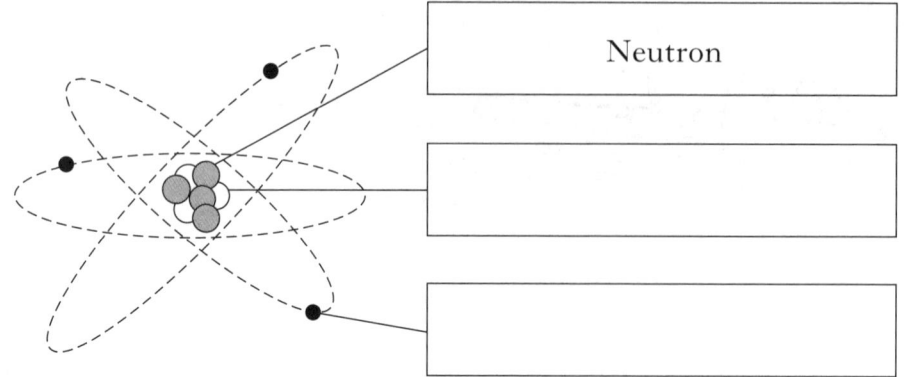

Neutron

1

(*b*) A radioactive source emits two types of radiation labelled R and S. The diagram shows how far these radiations will travel through different materials.

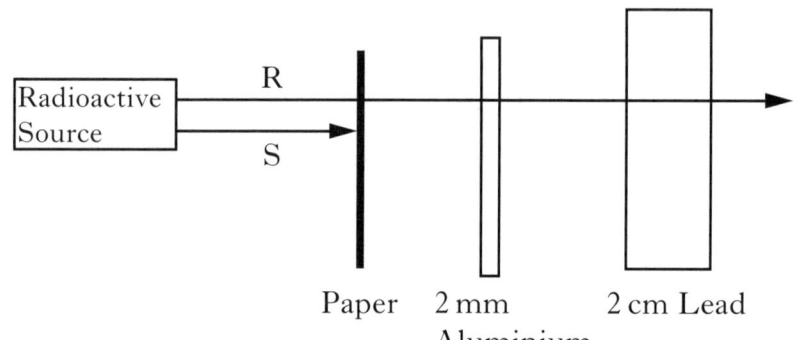

Radioactive Source

R

S

Paper   2 mm
Aluminium

2 cm Lead

(i)   Identify radiation R.

....

1

(ii) Identify radiation S.

....

1

(*c*) State **one** detector of nuclear radiation.

....

1

Marks

11. Different types of radiation can be used in medicine for both the diagnosis and treatment of a variety of illnesses.

The table shows information on some of the types of radiation used in medicine.

Type of radiation	Use of radiation
Infra red	
	Detects broken bones
Gamma	
	Treats skin conditions such as acne

(a) Complete the table to show:

   (i) the missing types of radiation; **1**

   (ii) the missing uses of radiation. **1**

(b) Lasers are also used in medicine for various treatments.

   (i) State **one** use of lasers in medicine.

   .... **1**

   (ii) Complete the diagram to show how light is transmitted along an optical fibre.

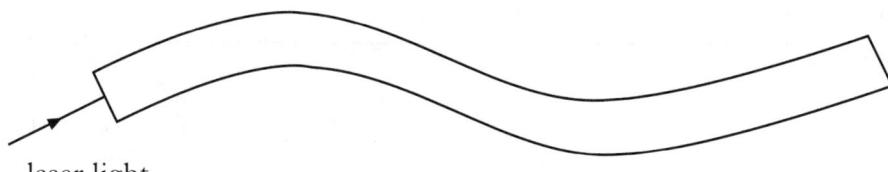

laser light

2

[Turn over

Marks

K&U | PS

12. An electronic megaphone is used by police to give instructions to large numbers of people.

A megaphone is a device that amplifies the voice of the person using it.

(a) The megaphone consists of an electronic system.

An electronic system can be represented by a block diagram.

The electronic devices used for the first two parts of the electronic system are shown below.

Complete the diagram by adding a suitable output device.

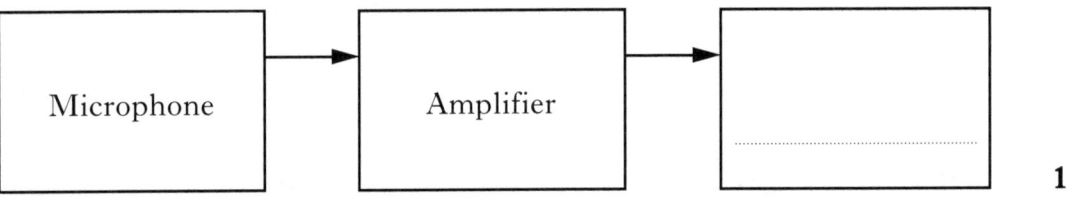

1

12. (continued)

(b) The megaphone is being tested.

Two oscilloscopes are used to display the signals from the microphone and from the output device.

For one test, the signal obtained from the output device is shown in Figure 2.

The settings for each oscilloscope are identical.

Complete Figure 1 to show the corresponding signal from the microphone.

Signal from microphone

Signal from output device

 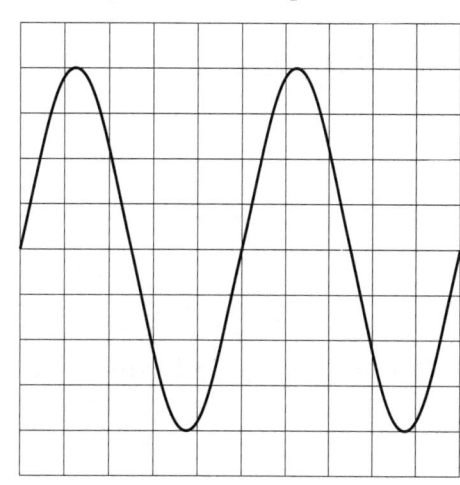

Figure 1   Figure 2   **2**

(c) During another test of the megaphone, the voltage measured at the microphone is 0·25 volts. The voltage measured at the output device is 2·25 volts.

Calculate the voltage gain of the amplifier.

Space for working and answer

2

13. An electronic circuit, used to give a warning, is shown below.

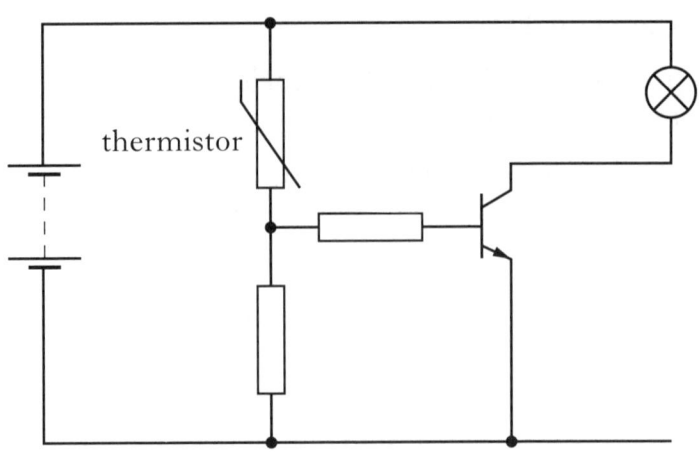

thermistor

(*a*) (i) What causes the resistance of a thermistor to change?

.... **1**

(ii) State the function of the transistor in this circuit.

.... **1**

(iii) How does the circuit indicate this warning?

.... **1**

(iv) Suggest where this circuit could be used to give a warning.

.... **1**

(*b*) Some electronic devices are listed below.

7 segment display   LED   Relay   Switch

Motor   Solar Cell   LDR   Solenoid

From the list, state **two** digital output devices.

....

.... **2**

Marks

14. A car of mass 1500 kilograms accelerates from rest to a speed of 18 metres per second in 6 seconds.

(a) Calculate the acceleration of the car.

> *Space for working and answer*

2

(b) The car now travels at a constant speed of 18 metres per second for a time of 5 minutes.

Calculate the distance travelled in this time.

> *Space for working and answer*

2

(c) The driver performs an emergency stop.

Explain in terms of forces how the seatbelt protects the driver.

....

....

2

15. In an experiment, a student times how long it takes to run up a flight of stairs in a school.

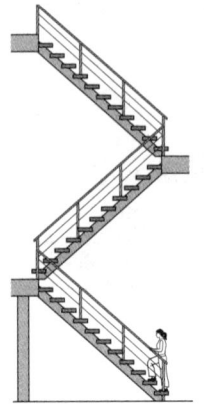

The student obtains the following data.

Mass of student	55 kilograms
Height of stairs	10 metres
Time to climb stairs	11 seconds

(*a*) Calculate the potential energy gained by the student at the top of the stairs.

> *Space for working and answer*

2

(*b*) Calculate the power developed by the student during the climb.

> *Space for working and answer*

2

Marks

DO NOT
WRITE IN
THIS
MARGIN

| K&U | PS |

15. **(continued)**

(*c*) At the top of the stairs, the student drops two identical sheets of paper down the stairwell.

One sheet is crumpled into a ball.

Both sheets are dropped from the same height at the same time.

Explain which sheet of paper will hit the ground first.

....

.... **2**

[Turn over

DO NOT
WRITE IN
THIS
MARGIN

K&U | PS

Marks

16. A family wishes to reduce the heat energy being lost from their house.

Heat energy can be lost from the house in three different ways: conduction, convection and radiation.

The family obtains an information booklet that gives advice on some methods to reduce heat loss from the house.

(a)	Fit draught-proofing strips to windows and doors.
(b)	Fit double glazing.
(c)	Increase the amount of loft insulation.
(d)	Fill the outside cavity walls with foam.
(e)	Reduce the height of all rooms with high ceilings.
(f)	Place aluminium foil behind the radiators.

(a) Select **one** method from the list that would:

   (i)   reduce heat lost by conduction;

       1

   (ii) reduce heat lost by convection.

       1

16. (continued)

(b) Three identical houses at different locations have a heating system that keeps the inside temperature at 19 degrees celsius.

The table gives the average outside temperature at each location.

House location	Average outside temperature in degrees celsius
Forfar	7
Braemar	4
London	11

(i) Which house location will have the greatest heat loss?

....

1

(ii) Give a reason for your answer.

....

1

(c) Three students carry out an experiment to investigate heat loss by radiation. They use three metal cubes which are different colours. The same volume of water at 80 degrees celsius is poured into each cube. The temperature of each cube is measured at regular intervals using an infrared thermometer as shown.

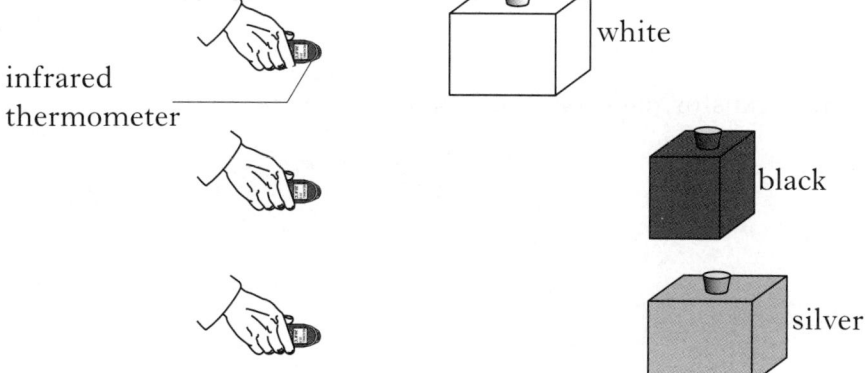

infrared thermometer

white

black

silver

State **two** reasons why this is not a fair test.

....

....

2

Marks

K&U	PS

17. Electricity can be generated from different energy sources.

(*a*) Examples of energy sources are:

gas   wind   oil   solar   wave   hydro   coal

These energy sources can be classified as renewable or non-renewable.

Complete the table below to show which of these examples are renewable and which are non-renewable.

Renewable	*Non-renewable*

2

(*b*) A coal-fired power station burns coal in order to generate electricity. A simplified diagram of a coal-fired power station is shown.

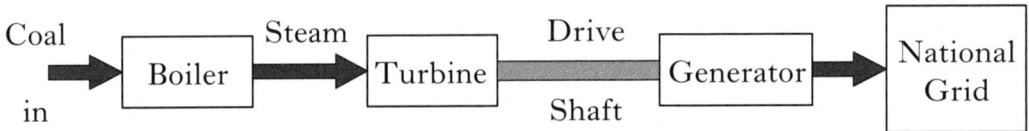

State the energy transformation in the boiler.

....

1

Marks

17. (continued)

(*c*) Drax power station is a coal-fired power station that can generate a power of 3960 megawatts.

Cruachan power station is a pumped hydro-electric scheme that can generate a power of 440 megawatts.

(i) How many pumped hydro-electric schemes would be required to generate the same power as Drax power station?

Space for working and answer

1

(ii) The pumped storage scheme uses water at the rate of 200 kilograms per second. The scheme can run continuously for 22 hours.

Calculate the mass of water that would pass through the scheme in this time.

Space for working and answer

1

[Turn over

18. Visible light is part of a family of waves known as the electromagnetic spectrum.

   (*a*) What is the speed of waves in the electromagnetic spectrum?

   ....   **1**

   (*b*) A student notices that when white light passes through a glass of lemonade it is split into different colours.

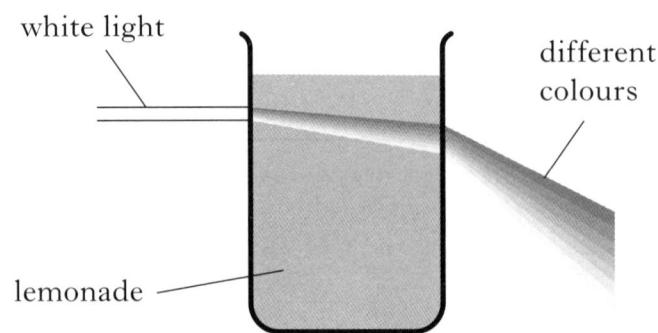

   The student decides to reproduce this effect in a laboratory using the following equipment.

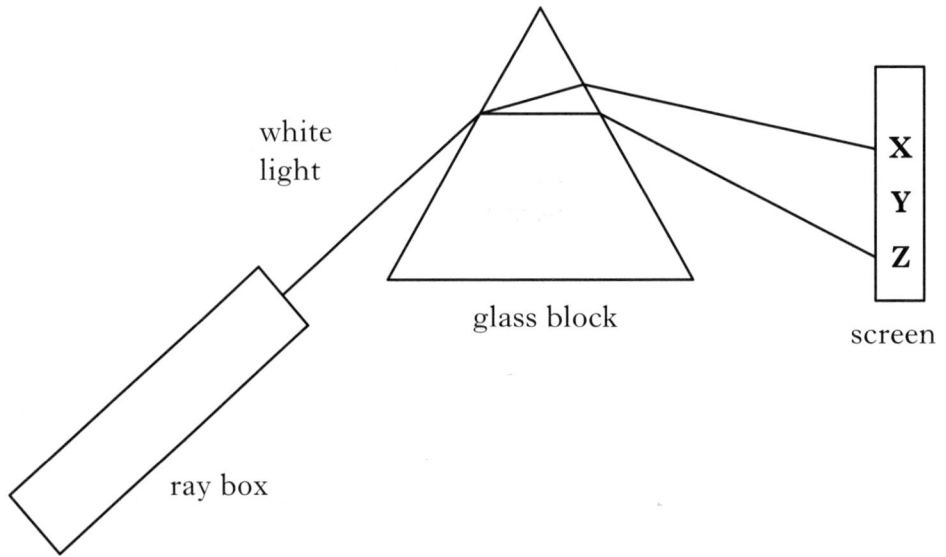

   (i) State the name of the glass block that the student uses to split the light into different colours.

   ....   **1**

Marks

18. (*b*) **(continued)**

(ii) When white light enters the glass block its speed and direction are changed.

What name is given to this effect?

....

1

(iii) The colours appear on the screen in order of wavelength. The shortest wavelength appears at Z.

State which of the colours green, blue or red would be seen at positions **X**, **Y** and **Z** on the screen.

X ....

Y ....

Z ....

2

[Turn over

19. In a science classroom, pupils make "rockets" by adding vitamin C tablets to water in a container.

The vitamin C tablet, attached to the lid, and the water react to give off a gas which causes the container to rise.

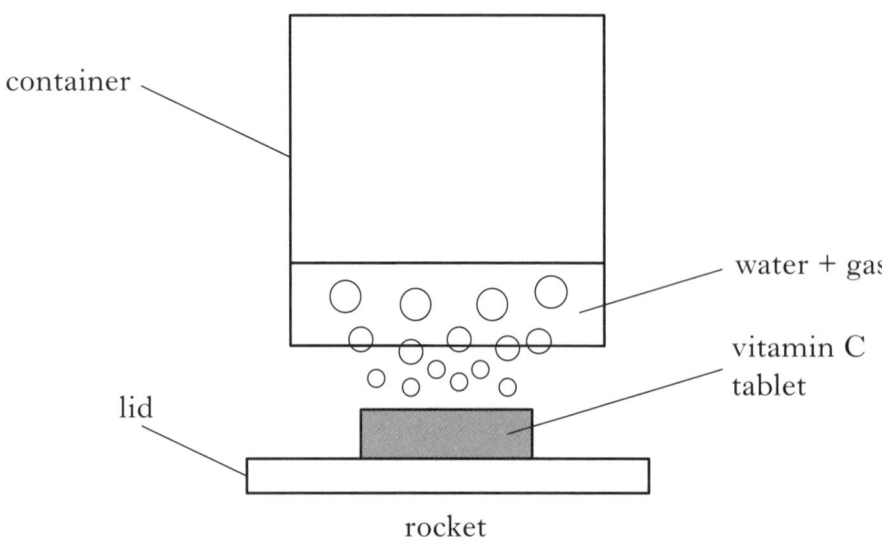

container

water + gas

vitamin C tablet

lid

rocket

(*a*) Complete the passage below, to make the statement correct.

As the container rises, it exerts a force downwards on the gas and water.

The _____ exerts a force

_____ on the container.   **1**

Marks

DO NOT
WRITE IN
THIS
MARGIN

K&U | PS

19. (continued)

(b) The container has a mass of 0·05 kilograms. The upward force on the container is 2 newtons.

(i) Calculate the weight of the container.

Space for working and answer

2

(ii) Calculate the unbalanced force acting on the container.

Space for working and answer

1

(iii) Calculate the acceleration of the container.

Space for working and answer

2

[END OF QUESTION PAPER]

ADDITIONAL SPACE FOR ANSWERS

Make sure you write the correct question number beside each answer.

DO NOT WRITE IN THIS MARGIN

K&U	PS

ADDITIONAL SPACE FOR ANSWERS

Make sure you write the correct question number beside each answer.

[BLANK PAGE]

DO NOT WRITE ON THIS PAGE

[BLANK PAGE]

Acknowledgements

Permission has been sought from all relevant copyright holders and Bright Red Publishing is grateful for the use of the following:

An image of ghd hair straighteners © ghd (2011 General page 10);

An image of two Citroën cars © PSA Peugeot Citroën (2011 General page 16);

A photo of a Honda Insight Eco Car © Honda (UK) (2012 General page 15).

STANDARD GRADE | ANSWER SECTION

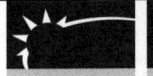

SQA STANDARD GRADE GENERAL PHYSICS
2008–2012

PHYSICS GENERAL
2008

1. A

2. C

3. D

4. D

5. C

6. (a) The **aerial** of a radio receiver detects signals from many different stations and converts them into electrical signals. The **tuner** selects one particular station from many. The **amplifier** increases the amplitude of these electrical signals. The energy required to do this is supplied by the **battery**. The loudspeaker in a radio receiver converts **electrical** energy into **sound** energy.

   (b) (i)   6 cm
       (ii)   3 cm

7. (a) (i)   increases (amplitude of) received signal
           or
           collects/gathers more signals
       (ii)

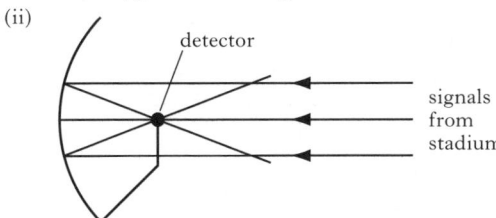

   (b) amplitude of signal is reduced

8. (a) variable resistor/resistance

   (b) heat from iron could melt flex

   (c) (i)   brown
       (ii)   safety device **or** prevents shock/ electrocution
       (iii)   requires more current **or** requires more power **or** more energy

9. (a)

	Lamp 1	Lamp 2
Current (amperes)	0·2	0·2
Voltage (volts)	6	6

   (b) 12 V

   (c) circuit 1

10. (a) (sound levels above 80dB) can damage hearing

   (b) (i)   People of all age groups can hear sound frequencies up to 10 or 12 kHz
           Hearing loss increases with age
           Hearing loss increases with frequency
       (ii)   ultrasound/ultrasonic

11. (a) 0·015A

   (b) (i)   electronic switch
       (ii)   warning provided **or**
           lamp lights/indicates when water temperature becomes too high

12. (a) (i)   *Any two from:*
           more accurate reading
           smaller range
           reading remains constant (until reset)
       (ii)   patient's temperature is above average or above normal

   (b) (i)   radium (–226) **or** alpha **or** 1600 years
       (ii)   technetium (–99) **or** gamma **or** 6 hours
       (iii)   technetium (–99) **or** gamma **or** 6 hours

13. (a) (i)   LDR
       (ii)   binary
       (iii)   seven-segment display

   (b)

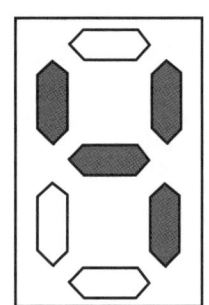

14. (a) 7200 m

   (b) 1·5 (m/s)

   (c) step length may vary

15. (a) (i)   2500 N
       (ii)   2500 N

   (b) 1800 J

   (c) use trolley **or** use rollers under piano **or** lubricate piano wheels

16. (a) (i)   light to electrical energy
       (ii)   32 W

   (b) (i)   (any value within range of) 16 W and 32 W
       (ii)   2·5 A

   (c) it may not be windy, it may not be sunny

17. (a) (i)   50
       (ii)   transformers only work with a.c. **or** transformers do not work with d.c. (**or** batteries)

   (b) In the National Grid, **step-up** transformers are used to increase the 25 000 volts from a power station to 132 000 volts for transmission. This reduces **energy/power loss** in the transmission lines. The voltage is then decreased to 11 000 volts for industry and 230 volts for domestic use using **step-down** transformers.

18. (a) (i)   5250 J
       (ii)   player's ankle

   (b) coolant changing state (or melting)

   (c) to reduce heat transfer **from** surroundings (not to reduce heat transfer **to** surroundings)

19. (a) (i)   Callisto **or** Ganymede **or** Europa **or** moon
       (ii)   a star/the sun and its planets

    (b) (i)   ions exert a forward force on ion drive engine
        (ii)   0·0025 metres per second per second

    (c) there are no frictional forces in space

20. (a) (i)

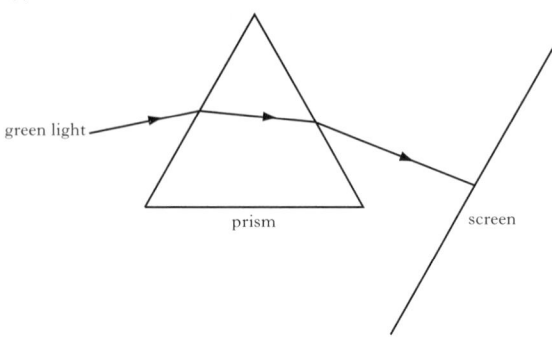

green light — prism — screen

       (ii)   visible spectrum or visible colours
       (iii)   any correct colour - red/orange/yellow

    (b) *Any one from:*
        • information about atoms (or elements) present
        • age of star
        • distance to star
        • speed of star
        • type of star
        • temperature of star

PHYSICS GENERAL
2009

1. C

2. B

3. B

4. C

5. A

6. C

7. (a) Electrical (energy) → Sound (energy)

   (b) Stations transmit in different places/areas/parts of Scotland
       OR
       Borders and Central are far enough apart (not to interfere)

   (c) (i)

   decoder → amplifier

       (ii) Selects/picks/finds: one frequency/radio
            wave/wavelength/(radio) station/ channel/signal/carrier
            wave

8. (a)   amplitude

   (b)

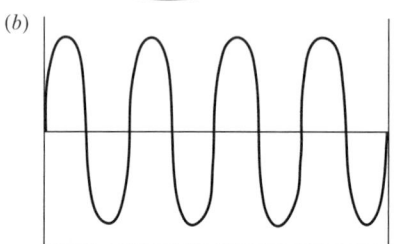

9. (a) I = 4·6 + 1·5
          = 6·1 amperes

   (b) Reading on ammeter goes down/reduces/decreases/falls (to
       1·5 A)

   (c) (i)   230   a.c.

       (ii)   50

10. (a) $R = \dfrac{V}{I}$

          $= \dfrac{24}{1·25}$

          $= 19·2\ \Omega$

    (b) $V = \dfrac{24}{16}$

          $= 1·5$ volts

    (c) (i) Join/connect/etc probes **and** lamp should light/see if
            the lamp lights

        (ii) Battery flat /voltage too low
             or broken/loose wire
             or open circuit
             or lamp faulty/broken
             or lamp short circuited

    (d) (i) A In the filament/wire
            B In the gas

        (ii) Discharge tubes are more efficient
             or cost less to run in the long term
             or more light for same power or converse
             or save energy
             or produce less heat (and more light)
             or lasts longer

11. (*a*) **same** speed
   or
   Travel at speed of light
   or
   Travel at 3×10^8 m/s
   / 300 000 000 m/s / 300 million m/s

   (*b*) Detect/find broken bones
   or take pictures/images of broken bones
   or CT scans
   or destroying tumours

   (*c*) (i) Gamma can be detected outside the body
   or alpha/beta are absorbed by the body
   or gamma rays are very/more penetrating

   (ii) Becquerels **or** Bq

   (*d*) Laser scalpel for cutting tissue
   or eye surgery
   or removing tattoos
   or (surface) tumour removal
   or remove birthmarks
   or sealing blood vessels etc

   (*e*) (i) different lens thickness
   or
   lens A thicker than lens B (or converse)
   or
   beads closer in B (or converse)
   or
   beads are at different distances
   or
   lenses are different sizes

   (ii) causes skin cancer
   or sunburn
   or skin damage
   or causes eye damage (eg cataracts)
   or kills skin cells

12. (*a*) (i) Piano

   (ii) $\lambda = \dfrac{v}{f}$

   $= \dfrac{340}{523}$

   $= 0.650$ metres

   (*b*) decibel **or** dB

13. (*a*) Buzzer
   or (loud)speaker
   or (alarm) bell

   (*b*) (i) (screen) 1

   (ii)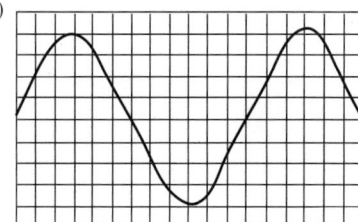

14. (*a*) (push) switch

   (*b*) AND

   (*c*) (i)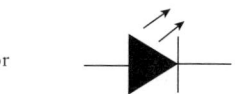

   (ii) Protect the LED
   or prevent damage to the LED
   or limits the current
   or reduces voltage <u>across</u> LED

   (*d*) 7 segment display
   or LCD
   or an array of LEDs

15. (*a*) Clear indication of the following:
   • Measure length/distance of **track/one lap**
   • Time (for) one lap
   • Use formula $v = \dfrac{d}{t}$ (to calculate average speed)

   or divide the distance by time

   (*b*) (i) Speed in metres per second (or m/s), time in seconds
   (or s)
   Uniform scales on both axes
   Correct plotting of t=4s, v=12m/s
   Straight line from origin to (4, 12)

   (ii) $a = \dfrac{v - u}{t}$ or $a = \dfrac{\Delta v}{t}$

   $= \dfrac{12 - 0}{4}$

   $= 3$ metres per second

   (*c*)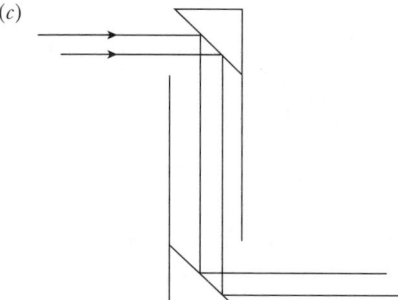

16. (*a*) 550 N **or** same as her weight

   (*b*) $E_W = F \times d$
   $= 550 \times 20$
   $= 11000$ joules

   (*c*) $P = \dfrac{E}{t}$

   $= \dfrac{11000}{40}$

   $= 275$ watts

   (*d*) Increase friction (between hands and wall)
   or
   reduces moisture (which causes slipping)
   or
   Increase grip
   or
   Stop slipping

17. (a) Conduction: double glazing
    Convection: loft insulation
    Radiation: foil-backed plasterboard

    (b) (0)6:00 or 6 am or '6 (o'clock) in the morning'

18. (a) (Fossil fuels) will run out
    or have a finite supply
    or are non renewable
    or cause pollution/greenhouse gases/global warming

    (b)

Renewable	Non-renewable
Hydroelectric	coal
Solar	gas
Wind	nuclear

    (c) (i) A generator
        B reactor

        (ii) Uses cheap off-peak power to store energy behind the dam for generating the next day (or similar)
        or
        The water is pumped back up into the upper reservoir to be reused (or similar)

        (iii) number of stations = $\dfrac{\text{total power}}{\text{power per station}}$

        $= \dfrac{1 \cdot 5}{0 \cdot 25}$

        = 6 (stations)

19. (a) Prism
    or grating
    or spectroscope
    or spectrometer

    (b) (i) Rigel **or** blue

        (ii) hotter

    (c) Any waves from EM spectrum except visible (light)

    (d)

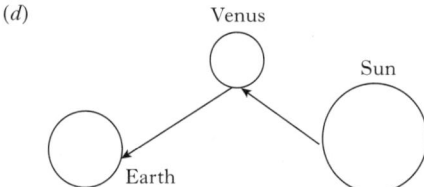

20. (a) Planet, Moon
    (b) Solar system, 8 minutes
    (c) The Sun, universe

---

1. D

2. A

3. C

4. D

5. B

6. (a) (i) f = $\dfrac{20}{10}$

        = 2 hertz

        (ii) v = f λ
        = 1·2 × 2
        = 2·4 metres per second

    (b) 2 × 0·15 = 0·3 metres

7. (a) Time (for signals to travel from satellites to sat nav)

    (b) Radio signals are waves which transfer ...**energy**... ...The radio signals travel at the speed of light, which is ...**greater**...... than the speed of sound... The period of a satellite orbit depends on its ...**height**...... above the Earth.

    (c)

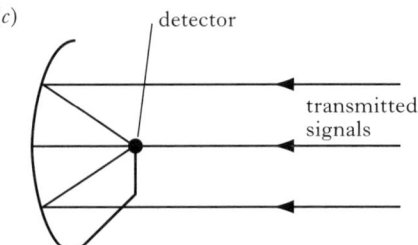

8. (a) (i) 0·2 ampere

        (ii) $\dfrac{12}{3}$
        = 4 volts

    (b) (i)

	Lamp 1	Lamp 2	Lamp 3
Voltage (volts)	4	4	8·0
Current (amperes)	0·2	0·2	0·4

        (ii) P = IV
        P = 0·4 × 8
        P = 3·2 watts

        (iii) electrical to light energy

9. (a) (i) t = $\dfrac{E}{P}$

        t = $\dfrac{14400}{48}$

        t = 300 seconds

        (ii) The current is in one direction

    (b) (i)

Appliance	Power (watts)
Kettle	2800
Bedside lamp	60
Cooker	8000

        (ii) The earth wire is a safety device

10. (a) (i) 0 decibels

(ii) Inside a classroom

(b) Loud sounds can damage hearing
or
Sounds above 80 dB can damage hearing
or
102 dB sounds can damage hearing
or
Can damage eardrum
or
Causes deafness

(c) (i) Ultrasound **or** ultrasonic

(ii) Obtaining images of unborn babies
or
removal of kidney stones
or
physiotherapy treatment

11. (a) less expensive
or
does not use hazardous chemicals
or
image obtained in a shorter time

(b) (i) Turns film black/dark
or
fogs
or
clouds film

(ii) x-rays are dangerous
or
for safety
or
to monitor radiation exposure
or
no digital eqivalent

(c) Infrared
or
IR
or
thermal

12. (a) (i) the voltage increases
or
'gets bigger'

(ii)

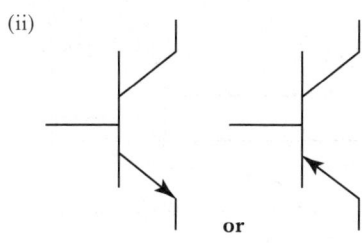

or

(iii) (Electronic) switch **or** 'to switch on the LED'

(b) (i) Reading increases
or
decreases
or
changes

(ii) $I = \dfrac{V}{R}$

$I = \dfrac{5}{1000}$

$I = 0.005$ ampere

13. (a) (i) LED connected the wrong way round

(ii) To protect the LED **or** limit the current in the LED
or reduce voltage across the LED

(b) (i)

Energy in	Output device	Energy out
electrical	**loudspeaker** OR **buzzer** OR **bell**	sound
electrical	LED	light
electrical	**motor** OR **moving coil meter** OR **solenoid**	kinetic
electrical	heater	heat

(ii) Buzzer
or
LED
or
solenoid
or
relay

14. (a) (Forces are) balanced
or
equal and in opposite directions

(b) $a = \dfrac{\Delta v}{t}$ **or** $a = \dfrac{v - u}{t}$

$= \dfrac{14}{2.5}$

$= 5.6$ metres per second per second

(c) $v = \dfrac{d}{t}$

$= \dfrac{720}{100}$

$= 7.2$ metres per second

15. (a) (i) It has wheels **or** rollers

(ii) To reduce the pulling force
or
make it easier to pull

(b) $E_w = Fd$
$= 20 \times 15$
$= 300$ joules

(c) (i) $E_p = mgh$
$= 16 \times 10 \times 0.4$
$= 64$ joules

(ii) $w = mg$
$= 16 \times 10$
$= 160 (N)$
No

16. (a) (i) Thermal $= 100 - 40 = 60$ (%)

(ii) $50 + 30 = 80$ (%)

(b) (i) Switch off lights
or
do not leave appliances on stand-by
or
fit draught proofing
or
use energy saving light bulbs

(ii) car share

or

use public transport

or

use more fuel efficient vehicles

17. (*a*) To change the size of the voltage

(*b*) (i) 132 000 volts

(ii) 33 000 volts

(iii) $\dfrac{n_s}{n_p} = \dfrac{Vs}{Vp}$

$\dfrac{n_s}{6000} = \dfrac{33000}{132000}$

$n_s = 1500$ (turns)

18. (*a*) Lens X   Eyepiece

Lens Y   Objective

(*b*) The Earth is turning

or

the Moon is moving

(*c*) Planet

Solar System

Galaxy

Universe

19. (*a*) (i) The water exerts an upward force on the air/rocket/bottle

(ii) $a = \dfrac{F}{m}$

$a = \dfrac{2\cdot1}{0\cdot70}$

$a = 3$ metres per second per second

(*b*) Gravitational pull is less than on Earth

or

Gravitational field strength is less

or

Weight (of rocket) is less

(*c*) (i) Weight

or

The force/pull of gravity

(ii) Friction

or

air resistance

or

drag

1. B

2. D

3. D

4. B

5. D

6. (*a*) d = vt

34 = v × 2·5

v = 13·6 (km/h)

(*b*) (i) $f = \dfrac{n}{t}$

$= \dfrac{8}{10}$

$= 0\cdot8$ Hertz

(ii)

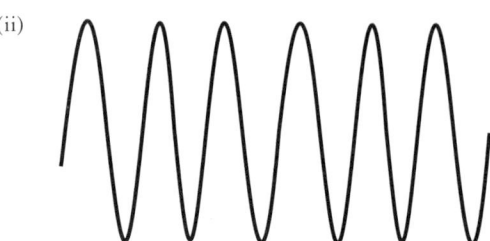

7. (*a*) (i) Lamp

(ii) $\begin{cases} \text{lamp is switched/flashed on and off} \\ \textbf{OR} \\ \text{switch is open and closed} \end{cases}$

according to an agreed code

(*b*) (i)

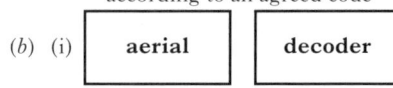

| aerial | decoder |

(ii) A Supplies electrical energy

B Selects one particular frequency/wavelength

8. (*a*)

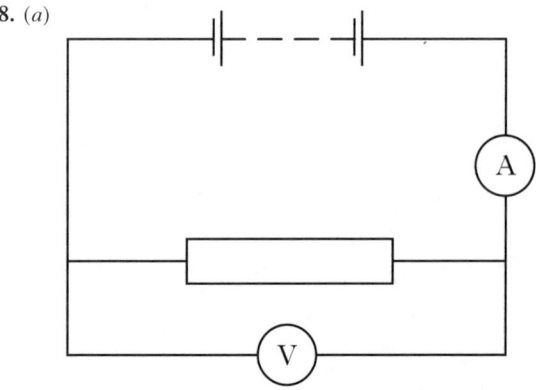

(*b*) (i) $R = \dfrac{V}{I}$

$= \dfrac{1\cdot5}{7\cdot5}$

$= 0\cdot2$ ohms

(ii) a decrease

9. (*a*) (i) Live and Neutral only

(ii) Live is brown

Neutral is blue

(b) $I = \dfrac{P}{V}$

$\quad = \dfrac{115}{230}$

$\quad = 0.5$ amperes

(c) (i) 3 amperes

   (ii) To protect the flex

10. (a) Liquid expands more than glass when heated

  (b) (i) Thermometer B

     (ii) Lowest recordable temperature is 35°C

      or

      Starts at around body temperature

      or

      Highest temperature is retained

      or

      Smaller temperature range

  (c) Recorded temperature is above **37 °C/normal body** temperature/ patient has a fever

11. (a) (i) Students are at different distances from the loudspeaker

     (ii) Ultrasound

  (b) *Any two from:*

    Bell: gathers/amplifies sound

    (Rubber) tubing: transmits sound from table/bell to student

    Earpieces: transfer sound to student's ears

    or

    excludes external sounds from student's ears.

12. (a) System B; both switches need to be closed before the output is logic level 1 and the door opening mechanism operates

  (b) System A; only one switch needs to be closed for the output to be logic level 1 and the doors open

13. (a) process

  (b) (i) thermistor

     (ii) seven-segment display

  (c) $V_{gain} = \dfrac{V_{out}}{V_{in}}$

       $= \dfrac{10}{0.4}$

       $= 25$

  (d) 1000 hertz

14. (a) (i) $F = ma$

        $= 800 \times 8$

        $= 6400$ newtons

     (ii) $E_w = Fd$

        $= 6400 \times 50$

        $= 320\,000$ joules

  (b) Not a fair test because cars may have different:

    braking systems

    or

    drag coefficients

    or

    Masses/weights/one car is heavier

15. (a) Change of speed per unit time/per second

    or

    Rate of change of speed

  (b) $a = \dfrac{\Delta v}{t}$ **or** $a = \dfrac{v - u}{t}$

     $= \dfrac{1.2 - 0}{0.001}$

     $= 1200$ metres per second per second

  (c) $W = mg$

      $= 0.0001 \times 10$

      $= 0.001$ newtons

16. (a) (i) Potential $\to$ Kinetic

     (ii) Kinetic $\to$ Electrical

  (b) (i) primary coil core   secondary coil

     (ii) $\dfrac{n_s}{n_p} = \dfrac{V_s}{V_p}$

       $\dfrac{n_s}{18000} = \dfrac{275000}{16000}$

       $n_s = 309375$

    (iii) To reduce the energy/power loss

17. (a) $E = P \times t$

     $= 25 \times 24$

     $= 600$ (kilowatt – hours)

  (b) Remaining energy $= 600 - 200$

                  $= 400$ (kilowatt – hours)

    cost of electricity $=$ No of kilowatt –hours

                       $\times$ cost per kilowatt – hour

                    $= 400 \times 9$

                    $= 3600$ pence

  (c) solar

    or

    wave

    or

    tidal

    or

    hydro

    or

    geothermal

    or

    biomass

    or

    Wood

18. (a) $F = ma$

    $4800 = 6000 \times a$

        $a = 0.8$ metres per second per second

  (b) (i) the same rate as

     (ii) friction

      or

      air resistance

      or

      drag

  (c) Point B

19. (a) (i) Miranda

      or

      Moon

(ii) Sun

or

Proxima Centauri

or

star

(iii) Proxima Centauri

(iv) Neptune/planet

or

Halley's comet

or

The Oort Cloud

(b) A group/collection of stars

(c) A star (or the Sun) and its planets

PHYSICS GENERAL 2012

1. A

2. C

3. D

4. B

5. A

6. (a) (i) microphone

   (ii) Sound to electrical energy

   (b) (i) B

   (ii) D

7. (a) wavelength $= \dfrac{\text{total distance}}{\text{number of waves}}$

   $= \dfrac{2 \cdot 5}{5}$

   $= 0 \cdot 5$ metres

   (b) $v = f\lambda$

   $= 2 \times 0 \cdot 5$

   $= 1$ metre per second

   (c) Energy is lost from wave as it moves

8. (a) $V = IR$

   $230 = 1 \cdot 25 \times R$

   $R = 184$ ohms

   (b) $E = Pt$

   $= 1 \cdot 6 \times 8 \times 7$

   $= 89 \cdot 6$ (kilowatt - hours)

   (c)

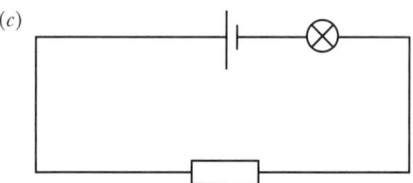

9. (a) In the filament **or** resistance wire

   (b) Less energy is transformed/changed into heat

   or

   more energy transformed/changed into light

   (c) $P = IV$

   $= 5 \times 12$

   $= 60$ watts

   (d) (i) Mains (electricity) supply/cable/socket/plug/ flex/appliance/kettle too close to water/sink/ tap

   (ii) Risk of shock/electrocution

10. (a)

proton(s)

electron(s)

   (b) (i) Gamma **or** γ symbol

   (ii) Alpha **or** α symbol

   (c) *Any one from:*

   • Geiger Muller tube

   • Photographic film

   • Film badge

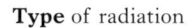

11. (*a*) (i)

Type of radiation
Answer: X-Rays (x rays)
Answer: Ultra violet **or** infra red

(ii)

Use of radiation
Answer: thermograms
Answer: treatment of cancer

(*b*) (i)· • Laser scalpel **or**
 • remove birth marks **or**
 • vapourise/treat tumours **or**
 • treat acne **or**
 • removal of tattoos **or**
 • eye surgery

(ii)

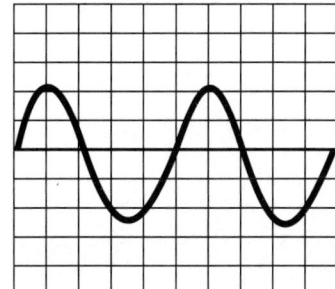

Laser light

12. (*a*) loudspeaker

(*b*) Signal from microphone

(*c*) Voltage Gain $= \dfrac{\text{voltage out}}{\text{voltage in}}$

$= \dfrac{2 \cdot 25}{0 \cdot 25}$

$= 9$ no unit

13. (*a*) (i) • Change **or**
 • Increase **or**
 • decrease in temperature/heat

(ii) electronic switch

(iii) Lamp will come on/go off

(iv) Any suitable application where temperature needs to be monitored is acceptable

(*b*) • 7 segment display **or**
 • LED **or**
 • relay **or**
 • solenoid

14. (*a*) $a = \dfrac{\Delta v}{t}$

$= \dfrac{18}{6}$

$= 3$ metres per second per second

(*b*) $d = vt$

$= 18 \times 5 \times 60$

$= 5400$ metres

(*c*) Seat belt exerts a decelerating force on the driver
This decelerates the driver

15. (*a*) $E_p = mgh$

$= 55 \times 10 \times 10$

$= 5500$ joules

(*b*) $P = \dfrac{E}{t}$

$= \dfrac{5500}{11}$

$= 500$ watts

(*c*) crumpled
will hit first as it is more streamlined
or
less **air** resistance

16. (*a*) (i) *Any one from:*
 • b: double glazing
 • c: loft insulation
 • d: cavity wall insulation

(ii) *Any one from:*
 • a: draught proofing
 • c: loft insulation
 • d: cavity wall insulation
 • e: reduce room height

(*b*) (i) Braemar

(ii) Temperature difference between the inside and the outside of the house is greatest
or
(Temperature) difference is 15°C

(*c*) the metal cubes are different:
 • sizes **or**
 • Volumes **or**
 • Shapes
the thermometers are at different distances from cubes

17. (*a*)

Renewable	Non-renewable
Wind	coal
Solar	oil
Wave	gas
Hydro	

(*b*) chemical to heat energy

(*c*) (i) number of schemes $= \dfrac{3960}{440}$

$= 9$ *schemes*

(ii) total mass of water $= 200 \times 22 \times 60 \times 60$
$= 15\,840\,000$ kg

18. (*a*) 300 000 000 metres per second **or**
3×10^8 metres per second

(*b*) (i) Prism

(ii) Refraction

(iii) X red
 Y green
 Z blue

19. (*a*) The <u>gas</u> **and** <u>water</u> exerts a force <u>upwards</u> on the container

   (*b*) (i) $W = mg$
$$= 0 \cdot 05 \times 10$$
$$= 0 \cdot 5 \text{ newtons}$$

      (ii) $F_{un} = \text{upward force} - \text{weight}$
$$= 2 - 0 \cdot 5$$
$$= 1 \cdot 5 \text{ newtons}$$

      (iii) $F_{un} = ma$
$$1 \cdot 5 = 0 \cdot 5 \times a$$
$$a = 30 \text{ metres per second per second}$$

Hey! I've done it

{BrightRED
PUBLISHING

© 2012 SQA/Bright Red Publishing Ltd, All Rights Reserved

Published by Bright Red Publishing Ltd, 6 Stafford Street, Edinburgh, EH3 7AU
Tel: 0131 220 5804, Fax: 0131 220 6710, enquiries: sales@brightredpublishing.co.uk,
www.brightredpublishing.co.uk

Official SQA answers to 978-1-84948-256-1
2008-2012